LENORMAND OF

Enchantment

Yasmeen Westwood

WRITTEN BY KALLIOPE

REDFeather™
MIND | BODY | SPIRIT
An Imprint of Schiffer Publishing, Ltd.

Library of Congress Control Number: 2021948657

"Red Feather Mind Body Spirit" logo is a trademark of Schiffer Publishing, Ltd.
"Red Feather Mind Body Spirit Feather" logo is a registered trademark of
Schiffer Publishing, Ltd.

Cover and interior design by Danielle Farmer
Type set in Desire/Minion

ISBN: 978-0-7643-6378-8
Printed in China
10 9 8 7 6 5 4 3 2

Published by REDFeather Mind, Body, Spirit
An imprint of Schiffer Publishing, Ltd.
4880 Lower Valley Road
Atglen, PA 19310
Phone: (610) 593-1777; Fax: (610) 593-2002
Email: Info@redfeathermbs.com
Web: www.redfeathermbs.com

Other REDFeather Titles by the Author:
The Tarot of Enchanted Dreams, Yasmeen Westwood, ISBN 978-0-7643-5828-9
Tarot of the Enchanted Soul, Yasmeen Westwood, ISBN 978-0-7643-6281-1
Hummingbird Wisdom Oracle Cards, Ellen Valladares, illustrations
by Yasmeen Westwood, ISBN 978-0-7643-6272-9

Other REDFeather Titles on Related Subjects:
Lenormand Cartomancy, Christopher Butler, ISBN 978-0-7643-4562-3
Lenormand Oracle Cards, Alexandre Musruck, ISBN 978-0-7643-5469-4
The Egyptian Lenormand, Nefer Khepri, ISBN 978-0-7643-4776-4

Contents

Acknowledgments

The first person I would like to acknowledge is Yasmeen Westwood, for the opportunity to pen words to her inspirational art. In October 2019 I answered Spirit's call, traveled across the pond, and met my soul sister . . . and the rest is history.

A special thank you to my friend Betty Jane Ware, who was instrumental for making my trip to the UK happen.

I also want to acknowledge my King of Swords, who always believed that I could, so I did.

A special shout out to my sister Eva, who has been my personal cheerleader. It is her special kind of magick that has shown me that anything is possible.

Very grateful to Spirit for always guiding me, as I follow my soul's path, allowing me the pleasure to do what I love everyday.

Welcome

Welcome to the wonderful world of the *Lenormand of Enchantment*; this is not your grandmother's deck!

We have taken the Lenormand world by storm and revolutionized the way the Lenormand system is read. Our goal is to bring the Lenormand back out of the dark ages into modern day with a fresh new look, with updated and relevant meanings. The goal of this deck is to be in league with and rival some of the best, preferred divination systems in use today. The *Lenormand of Enchantment* will do just that, bringing the Lenormand back in style! Our vision is that this deck will appeal to the masses and be in every professional's arsenal, with updated artwork, modern meanings, and combinations that are applicable to today's day and age, yet managing to hold on to a semblance of antiquity. The traditionalist won't be lost, and those new to the Lenormand system will be thrilled with the level of accuracy and inspired at the ease of interpretation. As a special mention, this guidebook was created during the time of the COVID-19 pandemic, and some of the writings were slightly influenced by that energy. This was done intentionally to immortalize history, like a mini time capsule of the dark times that united the world. My hope for this tiny spark of a deck is that it will find its way around the globe and bring a little bit of light to chase away the darkness.

All my love,
Kalliope

Introduction

What Is the Lenormand?

The Lenormand is a 36-card complete system of divination.
Being a very old system of divination, there is much dispute about dates and its historical origins. This guidebook is not the place to get into historical debates, for I chose to see the beauty that lies in the simple symbols within this system of cards, and how each of the cards speaks to each other and relates to one another. The Lenormand cards are read in pairs and strings, and their interpretation relies heavily on combined meanings of two cards to form one thought or sentence. Most of the cards have a distinct positive or negative connotation, while a few cards can be viewed as neutral.

The Lenormand

Misconceptions of the Lenormand

There are many people who feel that the Lenormand is an old, outdated system that has no relevance to today's modern world. With its outdated meanings and confusing "rules," it does not have the ability to answer questions or provide any sort of insight, and it is vague and hard to learn . . . and this my friends, cannot be further from the truth!

1. You need intuition to read the cards. The Lenormand is a "come as you are" deck; what you see is what you get, not shrouded in esoteric mystery. Intuition is not required but is most certainly welcomed.

2. The system is difficult to learn; with so many combinations and meanings it will impossible to memorize them all! The Lenormand is not about memorization; it is about understanding the keywords and knowledge of the cards' symbols.

3. The system is confusing; there are so many different styles of reading the cards. When first starting out, pick a system that makes sense to you, and stick with it.

4. The Lenormand and Tarot share some of the same symbols, and that makes them the same. Lenormand cards have no connection to Tarot cards and are not read in the same way, even if some cards share the same name. They are two completely separate divination systems. The biggest difference is that Lenormand is verbal while Tarot is visual.

5. I don't like the Lenormand because some of the cards are so negative and look scary! The Lenormand has positive, negative, and some neutral cards; that is just the way the Lenormand rolls, with the ups and downs of life.

These are just a few of the misconceptions that people have with the Lenormand. As you learn the language of the deck, you will be able to dispel many myths of your own.

Choosing Your Lenormand Deck

With so many decks and styles available today, make sure that you choose a deck with artwork that appeals to you. The colors and the imagery have to grab and hold your attention.

Storing Your Cards

This is strictly up to the individual; some choose pretty silk cloths, and others keep their decks in the original box. There is not a right or wrong way to store your cards; just do what feels right to protect your treasure.

Cleansing Your Cards

There are many ways to cleanse your cards if you feel called to do so; by far the easiest way is to put them in their numerological order.

How Can Lenormand Help?

Lenormand can help you get in touch with the intuitive, magickal side of yourself, by expanding your awareness, offering insight into your life, and clarifying any situation.

Discernment

When reading for others, you are responsible for what comes out of your mouth . . . PERIOD.

Fun Things to Do with the Lenormand

Journaling is key to self-discovery, learning the system by applying new meanings and discovering exciting new combinations. Many writers use the cards to get through creative blocks and inspire new plot twists. If you love to paint or draw, you can always pull out a card and create a version of your own. The possibilities are truly endless.

A Few Key Points and Practical Tips When Learning the Lenormand

- The Man and Woman cards are the significators and always represent the Seeker.

- The cards are read in pairs and strings. Each card is a word, and when you string a couple of cards together, they form a sentence.

- The meanings are not esoteric in nature; they are for everybody.

- There are no reversals in the Lenormand; all cards are read in the upright position.

- Playing card associations, known as "the pips," can "up" your Lenormand game. Just look to the bottom right corner to see which pip corresponds to each card.

- There are positive, negative, and neutral cards attached to each card's meaning.

- Each Lenormand card is equally important and carries the same weight.

- Lenormand cards have timing attached to each card, some more poignant than others, by using numerology or the generally accepted timing of that card.

- Cards are always read within the context of the question, and common sense is key when interpreting the Lenormand cards.

- The cards are metaphoric and can be read literally. Sometimes they present themselves as a humorous play on words and more often speak bluntly with a kind of "in your face" attitude.

- Order matters! What comes before and after? It is this nuance that makes all the difference in the interpretation of the cards.

- Spreads are not common with the Lenormand system. We leave that up to Tarot, where spreads are created with specific predetermined questions such as "What do I need to know about this situation?" or "Who or what will hinder me as I strive to achieve my goal?" These are just some examples; again, it's up to you to play and explore with your cards. Even though it's not common to use spreads doesn't mean that you cannot; we threw the rule book out the window with *The Lenormand of Enchantment*.

- The Lenormand is a great system when you need a clear answer to a question.

Beginning a Reading

STEP 1: Set the mood

Sometimes it's just as simple as taking three deep breaths to raise your vibration and go for it.

STEP 2: Shuffle your cards

Mix up the energy of the cards and shuffle until it feels right.

STEP 3: Ask your question

State your question either out loud or within. It doesn't matter, just as long as you are clear on what you are asking.

STEP 4: Selecting your cards and laying the cards

When you are ready, lay out your cards; pull as many or as few as you like, as long as you pull more than one card.

STEP 5: Interpreting the cards

First take a moment to observe which cards came out, and turn to the page in your guidebook for that card.

STEP 6: Closing

Take a moment to thank your cards for the wisdom imparted, take a couple of grounding breaths, and put the cards away.

The Lenormand of Enchantment is written and illustrated in a way that will keep giving you gems of wisdom and impart secrets along the way, but only when you are ready to receive the messages.

Card Descriptions and Combinations

Let me introduce you to the language of the Lenormand. I channeled each card's energy into a little poem to be used as a mnemonic, so you can get to know each other a little better. I have included an extensive list of two-card combinations to help you get started on this enthralling journey.

When the enchantment of this deck swirls and weaves its words around you, you too will discover new and exciting combinations and meanings to add to your repertoire.

1 Rider

On a trusty steed I ride, bringing tidings from afar
News of a sad nature, or a wish from a shining star
Heralding the arrival of a Suitor, looming in the distance
Speedy is the Rider, changing direction in an instant

KEYWORDS

News, Announcements, Comings and goings, Delivery, Mobile, Visit, Speedy, Arrival, the Other Man, Young Man, a Suitor, a Broadcast, Mail, Parcel, Movement, Fast, Quick, Active, Notification, Visitor, Guest, Looming on the horizon, On the way!

MEANING

When the Rider arrives in a reading she is heralding something coming into your life, whether that will be a person, news, a delivery, or an announcement of sorts.

Lenormand Rider Combinations

2 CLOVER: Lucky encounter, lucky news, informal visitor, casual visit, fleeting encounter, chance meeting with a suitor, brief visit, betting on horses, informal announcement, casual movements

3 SHIP: Travel-related news, coming and goings, distant news, international news, directional movement, overseas visitor, shipment, international visitor, traveling, foreign suitor

4 HOUSE: Domestic news, houseguest, family newsletter, real estate announcement, housing notice, family is coming to visit, relative arrives

5 TREE: Health news coming, spiritual connection with a suitor, physiotherapy, patiently waiting for a delivery to arrive, extended visit, patiently waiting for an announcement

6 CLOUDS: Confusing announcement, sad news arrives, chaotic movement, ominous news, the storm is coming, confusing activity, disturbance is looming on the horizon, hiding the Other Man

7 SNAKE: Cheating with the Other Man, the Other Woman arrives, toxic visitor, complications arise, devious woman visits, jealous suitor

8 COFFIN: Final announcement, no news, no movement, ending a visit quickly, bad news, ending it with the Other Man, death of a young man, final visit, calling it quits with a suitor, death is looming on the horizon, no delivery, bad visit

9 BOUQUET: Invitation is received, wonderful news, cheerful announcement, good-looking suitor, sweet young man, show pony, surprising announcement, impromptu visit, enjoying the visit

10 SCYTHE: Unexpected guest, breaking news, blindsiding announcement, dangerous suitor, danger is looming on the horizon, unexpected news, dangerous movements, cutting off the Other Man, hurtful news, broken young man, breaking in a horse

11 WHIP: Arguing with the Other Man, aggressive visitor, quickie, getting to know a suitor, habitual movements, sexy young man, sexual relations with the other man, exercise, disruptive news, competing with the other man, repetitive movements

12 BIRDS: Couple comes to visit, gossipy news, talking to a suitor, telegram, nervous movements, verbal announcement, nervous suitor, unsettling news, flight arriving (arrivals), two of something is delivered, nervous visitor

13 CHILD: New news, new beginning, short visit, immature suitor, younger man, small announcement, gender-reveal announcement, new announcement

14 FOX: Employment news, work suitor, propaganda, sneaky movements, superficial suitor, manipulative other man, cunning visitor, job posting, suspicious announcement, fake news

15 BEAR: Big news, forceful visitor, powerful broadcast, huge announcement, powerful young man arrives, mother or grandmother coming for a visit, forced visit, something big is looming on the horizon, overbearing suitor

16 STARS: Hopeful news, online suitor, inspiring news, electricity comes on, goals manifest quickly, online news, positive announcement, motivating news, amazing news, technological advancements

17 STORK: A birth announcement, commuting, change will happen fast, seasonal visitor, change is on the horizon, pregnancy announcement, stork brings a delivery (baby news), relocation, seasonal announcement

18 DOG: Help is on the way, friendly visit, helpful news, friendly announcement, sympathetic suitor, watching the news, trustworthy young man, supportive friend, following someone's movements (stalking)

19 TOWER: Official news, formal declaration, past suitor arrives, legal motion, political movement, established suitor, lonely man, government announcement, arrogant visitor, legal disclosure, official announcement

20 GARDEN: Social-media news feed, public announcement, public movement, rendezvous with a suitor, group notification, public social-media post, socially active

21 MOUNTAIN: Holding off on an announcement, putting off a visit, obstacles on the horizon, stubborn other man, blocking off access, delayed delivery, restricted news, blocking movement

22 PATHS: Multiple guests, choices are presented, unfamiliar visitor, possibilities arise, indecisive young man, multiple deliveries, choices ahead, multiple announcements, multiple suitors, strange announcement

23 MICE: Worrying news, damaging announcement, lost parcel, stressful news, diminished movement, lost notification, dirty young man

24 HEART: Relationship is announced, love is on the horizon, love comes in a hurry, kind visitor arrives, dating post or ad, love arrives, loving announcement, a lover

25 RING: Marriage or engagement announcement, offer arrives, deal closes quickly, promise is declared, married suitor, the contract arrives, circulating news

26 BOOK: Educational news, factual news, secret news, secret movements, wise announcement, information is delivered, book publishing, book report, informative news, smart announcement, secret visit, mysterious suitor

27 LETTER: Delivery of a parcel, letter arrives, package is arriving soon, written announcement, delivered message, message from the other man, text message arrives, results come in, messaging with a suitor

28 MAN: Flamboyant man, male visitor or caller, man arrives, the Other Man, news about a man, male suitor, attractive young man

29 WOMAN: Colorful lady, female visitor or caller, woman arrives, news about a lady, female admirer, attractive young lady

30 LILY: Retirement announcement, old news, slow things down and take your time, peace is on the way, long-awaited news, mature young man, winter is coming, private announcement

31 SUN: Good news, happy announcement, courageous young man, good tidings on the horizon, good mobility, wonderful visit, success is on the way, optimistic young man, warm tidings arrive

32 MOON: Emotional news, ebb and flow, comings and goings, intuitive flash, creative period ahead, nightly news, intuitive young man

33 KEY: Headline news, significant news, important announcement, significant young man, karma is coming, distinguished visitor, prominent suitor, notable announcement, key young man arrives, important visit

34 FISH: Financial news, money movement (coming in and going out), business announcement, money transfers, cash on delivery (COD), business-related news, money is on the way!

35 ANCHOR: Stability is on the way, settling down, safety announcement, reassuring news, routine visit, seahorse, serious announcement, stable young man, routine movement

36 CROSS: Difficult announcement, disappointing news, religious movement, obligated visit, difficulty moving around, critical announcement, crucial news, taxes arrive, offended by the other man, religious guest, regretting the announcement

When there's an elephant in the room, introduce him.
—Randy Pausch

2 Clover

In a lush green field, hidden I will grow
Lady Luck shinning, small riches I bestow
Grasp this moment of chance, for it will not last
A brief opportunity, that is soon to be in the past

KEYWORDS:
Luck, Short term, Small opportunity, Chance, Gamble, Informal, Small gain, Small happiness, Spontaneous, Quickness, Ease, Carefree, Lighthearted, Fleeting, Temporary, Casual, Comical, Fun, Cheerful

MEANING:
The Clover always brings luck, but it's fleeting. When the Clover appears, it can bring a surprising twist of fate, or an unexpected opportunity.

Lenormand Clover Combinations

1 RIDER: News brings a small opportunity, arrival of an opportunity, bit of luck, announcement comes quickly, lighthearted news, arrival of luck, visit does not last long

3 SHIP: Foreign gamble, exploring an opportunity, travel opportunity, your ship has come in, long-distance opportunity

4 HOUSE: Branding opportunity, family fun, real estate luck, small real estate opportunity, comfortable living, house of cards

5 TREE: Health improves, won the DNA lottery, spiritual opportunity, patience pays off, growth comes easy, healthful opportunity, healthful sense of humor

6 CLOUDS: Clouded luck, confusing opportunity, uncertain risk, hidden gambling, depression is temporary, sadness is short lived, confusion passes, a silver lining

7 SNAKE: Be wary of an opportunity, the allure of the game, complication arises, lies come easy, caution, there is a snake in the grass, attraction does not last, cheating at a game

8 COFFIN: Bad luck, end of a lucky streak, the outcome is unlucky, no chance, taking a final gamble, final opportunity, last chance, buried treasure, losing a game

9 BOUQUET: Good luck, something wonderful, perfect outcome, beautiful surprise, happy result, grateful for an opportunity

10 SCYTHE: Sudden stroke of luck, taking a dangerous chance, risk vs. reward, sudden opportunity, risky gamble, very quick

11 WHIP: Getting lucky, sex games (role play), sexual opportunity, hitting the jackpot, sexual excitement, sporting games, brief argument, repetitive gambling

12 BIRDS: Gossip is lighthearted, double dealing, conversation comes easy, excited energy, anxiety is temporary, exciting opportunity

13 CHILD: Small gamble, little luck, small window of opportunity, playing a game of chance, beginners luck, small chance, childish humor, playing games

14 FOX: Manipulating an opportunity, misleading luck, professional gambler, job opportunity, workplace fun, sleight of hand, fraudulent opportunity

15 BEAR: Big windfall, taking a big chance, powerful opportunity, forcing luck, immense gamble, big gain, weight gain

16 STARS: Wish comes true, very good luck, positive opportunity, online gaming, shining luck, high roller, dream opportunity, high stakes, online gambling, goals come easy, very likely chance

17 STORK: Change creates a small opportunity, change is temporary, change is positive, change comes easy, move is temporary, recurring opportunity

18 DOG: Friendship comes easy, trust is fleeting, support is temporary, friendship opportunity, friendship is brief

19 TOWER: Official lottery, casino, loneliness subsides, legal luck, past opportunity, rules of the game, established luck, litigation luck, ambitious opportunity

20 GARDEN: Social-gathering fun, party fun, group opportunity, meeting by chance, a social club

21 MOUNTAIN: A blocked opportunity, remote opportunity, tough luck, hinderance, poker face

22 PATHS: Unusual opportunity, decision is a gamble, double-dealing, multiple chances, planning to have fun, the choice is easy

23 MICE: Diminished luck, stress caused by gambling, losing the game, losing an opportunity, stolen opportunity, ruining your chances

24 HEART: Relationship bliss, relationship opportunity, love is a gamble, light-hearted fun, love at first sight, love does not last

25 RING: Marriage possibility, roulette, golden opportunity, "round and round she goes, where she stops nobody knows," the wheel of fortune, deal is a gamble, contract comes easy, continuing luck

26 BOOK: Educational opportunity, hidden possibility, knowledge comes easy, secret gambler, a bookie, secret opportunity, remember to have fun, researching an opportunity

27 LETTER: List of opportunities, results of the game, bucket list, lottery ticket, written rules of the game, message is cheerful, communication is temporary

28 MAN: The gambler, lucky man, risk-taker, Irish man, casual man, happy-go-lucky man, lighthearted man, funny man, an exciting man

29 WOMAN: Lady luck, gambling woman, risk-taker, Irish woman, casual woman, happy-go-lucky women, lighthearted woman, funny lady, an exciting woman

30 LILY: Retirement is carefree, experience brings ease, winter fun, old opportunity, winter opportunity, experienced gambler or gamer

31 SUN: Successful gamble, brilliant opportunity, hot winning streak, real chance, fearless gambler, good fortune, warmth is fleeting, great outcome, a win-win situation, good luck, winning the lottery, golden opportunity, good times

32 MOON: An intuitive flash, creativity comes easy, feeling spontaneous, feeling lighthearted, creative opportunity, emotional gambler

33 KEY: A door opens, key opportunity, significant small gain, access is brief, an open bet, unlocking an opportunity

34 FISH: Business gamble, temporary business opportunity, investment speculation, spending spree, the lure of gambling, investment is a gamble, resources do not last

35 ANCHOR: Lasting luck, solid opportunity, taking a serious chance, stability is short lived, safe bet, routine opportunity

36 CROSS: Disappointing luck, hardship caused by gambling, taking a crucial chance, painful game is played, regretting the gamble

Good Luck has its storms. —George Lucas

3 Ship

With billowing sails I travel, from lands afar
A destined journey I make, searching for my North Star
Adventures and voyages, navigating the high rolling sea
I was a wandering lost soul, when fate led you to me

KEYWORDS:

Travel, Movement, Goodbye, Distance, Transportation, Journey, Direction, Trade, Adventures, Overseas, Near the sea, Overseas, International, Navy, Abroad, Cruise, Far from home, Departures, Foreign, Navigation

MEANING:

The Ship is always about a journey and implies distances. The Ship is representative of all kinds of travel (long or short), all modes of transportation, and any moving vehicles.

Lenormand Ship Combinations

1 RIDER: News about a trip, adventure abroad, riding the waves, suitor leaves for good, announcing a trip, visitor from abroad, rushed goodbye

2 CLOVER: Lucky trip, happy journey, informal trip, smooth sailing, casual goodbye, chance voyage, spontaneous trip

4 HOUSE: Houseboat, homesick, house abroad, domestic travel, based abroad, house near water, relative leaves, far away trip

5 TREE: Spiritual journey, health-related trip, extended travel, health retreat, going in a healthful direction

6 CLOUDS: Stormy sea, uncertain journey, vague goodbye, sad trip, obscure trip, unsettled weather, a head trip, hidden movement, fear of travel, trouble is brewing on the sea, chaotic trip

7 SNAKE: Problematic trip, complicated journey, allure of travel, flexible movement, toxic trip, foreign lady, train, tube or subway

8 COFFIN: Final destination, last transition, bad trip, canceled trip, bad direction, no movement, final goodbye, completing a move, culminating movement

9 BOUQUET: Beautiful foreign land, travel upgrade, spa trip, nice goodbye, spring departure, going in a wonderful direction, surprise trip, journey east

10 SCYTHE: Last-minute travel, dangerous direction, accident during travels, dangerous journey, abrupt goodbye, dangerous movement, unexpected trip, cutting your travels short, autumn departure

11 WHIP: Exhausting trip, sports-related travel, sexually adventurous, repetitive travel, making a move (sexually), sex tourism, avid traveler

12 BIRDS: Discussing a journey, passengers, verbal directions, departures, a plane, saying goodbye, flight departs (departures), nervous traveler, curious explorer, hectic trip

13 CHILD: New adventure, small trip, making small movements, new direction, new country, fresh start, exploration, making small waves, inexperienced traveler, new car

14 FOX: Job in travel and tourism, sneaky movements, insincere goodbye, manipulative foreigner, suspicious movements, working far from home

15 BEAR: Power move, forced to travel, catering truck, forced to move, forced goodbye, a food truck, making big waves

16 STARS: Positive direction, a starship, internet, GPS, astral travel, OnStar (navigation), high seas

17 STORK: Moving for a fresh start, transferring, moving abroad, change of travel plans, moving away from home, changing planes, trains or buses, bohemian lifestyle

18 DOG: Follow directions, friendly goodbye, helpful foreigner, reliable vehicle, investigating a foreigner, someone is watching your moves, porter, bellman, concierge

19 TOWER: Official trip, formal goodbye, a consulate, official direction, organized travel, structured voyage

20 GARDEN: Social trip, group travel, team movement, public goodbye, networking abroad, group of foreigners, crowded destination

21 MOUNTAIN: International borders, blocked movement, putting off a goodbye, stagnation, delayed travel, rough seas, stubborn foreigner, restricted travel

22 PATHS: Multiple trips, choice of travel route, choosing to leave, going multiple directions, road trip, choosing a destination, unusual trip

23 MICE: Theft during a trip, costly trip, less movement, repairs to your car, losing your direction, ruined travel plans, less travel

24 HEART: Passionate about travel, the "Love Boat," attracted to foreigners, love for foreign lands, heartfelt goodbye, the love of travel, romantic cruise, romantic getaway

25 RING: Round trip, motorcycle, bicycle, wedding overseas, "90-Day Fiancé" visa, connecting flights, an offer to travel, continuous movement

26 BOOK: Studying abroad, educational trip, secret getaway, a passport, secret trip, unknown destination

27 LETTER: Letter in transit, itinerary, written goodbye, messaging someone internationally, postcard, texting someone goodbye, written directions

28 MAN: Foreign man, male traveler, worldly man, vagabond, ship's captain, male gypsy, jet-setter, male that works in travel and tourism

29 WOMAN: Foreign woman, female traveler, international woman, ship's captain, female gypsy, jet-setter, bohemian, female that works in travel and tourism

30 LILY: Veteran, older traveler, experienced traveler, long trip, a "snow bird," retirement trip, peaceful voyage, discreet farewell, winter departure, smooth sailing

31 SUN: Vacation, fun in the sun, tropical country, successful trip, bon voyage, moving in a good direction, warm farewell, summer departure, good trip, holiday travel

32 MOON: Emotional journey, emotional trip, emotional departure, emotional goodbye, journey into the abyss, overnight trip, traveling at night

33 KEY: Important movement, fated trip, destiny of the soul, open to direction, revealing travel plans, significant goodbye, important trip, distinguished foreigner

34 FISH: Fishing trip, fishing boat, in deep water, booze cruise, financial move, business venture, shopping trip, business trip, money transfer, financial trade, trade (import/export)

35 ANCHOR: Long journey, cruise ship, safe travels, a harbor, moored boat, parked car, reaching your destination, a safe direction, stuck abroad, routine travel

36 CROSS: Painful journey, cumbersome movement, disappointing trip, regretting the trip, overbooked trip, ill-fated trip, obligated travel, difficult journey, painful goodbye

I can't change the direction of the wind, but I can adjust my sails to always reach my destination. —Jimmy Dean

4 House

A House holds energy, in every nook and every wall
Welcome to come and stay awhile, tea is ready to pour
A comfortable sanctuary, familiar memories that remain
Families may look different, but the bond is just the same

KEYWORDS:
Home, Family, Real estate, Property, Comfortable, Relative, Sanctuary, Familiar surroundings, Domestic affairs, Indoors, Brand, Home page, Small buildings, Refuge, Shelter, a Place

MEANING:
"Home is where the heart is." —Pliny the Elder
The perfect way to describe the House card of the Lenormand. The House card represents your home, your family, relatives, and any others that are welcomed within its walls.

Lenormand House Combinations

1 RIDER: News regarding a house, guesthouse, coming and goings of the household, visitor arrives at your house, arrival of a roommate, coming home, suitor close to home

2 CLOVER: Short-term house rental, temporary housing, fun and carefree family, positive energy in the home, "The House" (casino), lucky family, happy home

3 SHIP: Far away from home, boathouse, foreign place, seaside home, leaving home, garage, traveling with the family, cruise ship, yacht

5 TREE: Healthy family, multigenerational family, ancestry (DNA), nursing home, growing family, spiritual family, log cabin, tree house, a grow-op, health spa

6 CLOUDS: Confusion surrounding a family member, chaotic household, addicted to real estate, unclear branding, disturbance within the home, turmoil in the family, madhouse, troubled family

7 SNAKE: Betrayal by someone close to you, plumbing or wiring problems in the home, toxic household, beware there is a snake behind closed doors, problems in the home

8 COFFIN: Funeral home, death in the family, a hospice, no family, a haunted house, the end of a family dynamic, burying a family member, a negative family, a vacant house

9 BOUQUET: Aesthetically pleasing home, greenhouse, spring cleaning, sweet-smelling house, well-kept home, pride in ownership, decorating a house

10 SCYTHE: Terminating a real estate deal, separated family, divorce in the family, cutting family ties, broken home

11 WHIP: Violence in the home, active household, critical family member, a bordello, arguments in the home, abusive family, competitive family, questioning a family member, abusive family member, abuse in the home

12 BIRDS: Siblings, roommates or flatmates, birdhouse, conversations about the house, negotiating real estate, ungrounded family member, nervous family member

13 CHILD: New house, children in the home, small house (tiny house), day-care, child's bedroom, childhood home, starter home, small family, new place, a playhouse

14 FOX: Manipulative family member, careful with real estate, working from home, working with family, suspicious family member, untrustworthy relation, your work family, unsavory neighborhood, manipulating the real estate market

15 BEAR: Powerful family, strong family values, restaurant, well-built house, the mother or grandmother of the family, powerful brand, overbearing family member, matriarchal family, the pantry, a big family

16 STARS: Dream home, blessed family, home page (social media), smart home (technology), harmonious household, astrological houses, celebrity home

17 STORK: Change of residence (moving house), the nursery, changes in the family, seasonal home, changes in the house, rearranging the house, nesting, moving away from home, remodeling

18 DOG: Pets in the home, neighbors or (your) neighborhood, friend of the family, tenants, alarm system, friend's house, the doghouse

19 TOWER: Hotel, fortified house, multiresidential building, isolated family, formal residence, traditional family, arrogant family member, head of household, rules of the house, established household, shunned family member

20 GARDEN: Public house, communal living, public family, landscaping, the backyard, home garden, camping, social family, public property

21 MOUNTAIN: Permanent home, estranged family member, base camp, stubborn family member, distant relative, blocked real estate, distant family member

22 PATHS: Choices involving the family, multiple home ownership, decisions about the house, choosing a home, row houses, alternative family

23 MICE: Destroying the house, decaying home (termites), damaged house, dirty house, a rat's nest, downsizing (house), repairs needed on the house

24 HEART: Cherished home; loving family, love shack, welcoming, warm home, the furnace, the hearth (fireplace), kind, charitable family, love lives here, falling in love with a property

25 RING: Bonded family, marital home, circle of trust (of family), offer on the house, committed family, honorable family, tight-knit family, dedicated to the family, contract on the property

26 BOOK: A secret family, library, student housing, researching houses (real estate), educated family, secret pad, secretive family member

27 LETTER: Title deed of the house, documents involving the house, message from a family member, listing a house

28 MAN: Family man, man of the house, male family member, male relative, man with strong family values, lord of the manor, homeowner, homeboy, handyman

29 WOMAN: Nurturer, the lady of the house, female family member, housekeeper, landlady, female relative, female with strong family values, lady of the manor, homeowner, homegirl

30 LILY: Peaceful home, patriarchal family, father or grandfather of the family, calm energy in the home, older home, grandparents of the family, old-age home, well-lived-in home, retirement home, an old family, private property

31 SUN: Joyful home, summer home, thriving family, a good house, successful family, vacation home, bright home with lots of light, successful brand, solarium, happy home

32 MOON: Intuitive family, magickal house, creative energy, art studio, music studio, emotional family member

33 KEY: Respected family, actual key to the house, portal in the house (energy), open house (real estate), "Say Yes! to" the house, an open family, getting the keys to a house, a prestigious brand, an unlocked door, distinguished family member

34 FISH: Pub or cocktail lounge, affluent family, investment property, purchase or sale of a home, mortgage, buying things for the house, fluctuating property values, assets of the house, alcoholic family member, cottage or cabin

35 ANCHOR: Waterfront property, cottage, lighthouse, stable home, safe house, harbor, stagnant energy in the home, safe neighborhood

36 CROSS: A memorial, regretting the purchase of a home, difficult family member, burdened family member, a spirit in the house, burdened by a house, obligated by a family member, a religious family

We shape our dwellings, and afterwards our dwellings shape us.
—Winston Churchill

5 Tree

Lush leaves and Tree branches, DNA that runs so deep
Precious vitality and blood ties, of the life force we seek
Extended time and spirituality, a delicate balance we try to hold
Roots reaching deeply into the earth, with the hope of growing old

KEYWORDS:

Health, Systems, of an extended time, Ancestors, Living, Well-being, Vitality, Natural, Medical, Spirituality, Blood ties, Growth, Deeply rooted, Essence, Vigor, DNA, Life, the Body, Spiritual connections

MEANING:

When the Tree appears it is almost always connected to health and well-being. When looking at any situation, the Tree is indicative of something that has taken root a while ago, has been slowly developing over time, and is now coming into fruition.

Lenormand Tree Combinations

1 RIDER: News about health, feeling better soon, quick recovery, suitor is taking their time, speedy recovery, mobility, arrival of vitality and well-being

2 CLOVER: Small improvement in health, informal diagnosis, lucky in life, opportunity is growing, the game of life, lucky outcome in a health situation, brief recovery, chance to network, the funny bone

3 SHIP: Health-related voyage, travel sickness, car repair, ride in an ambulance, trip is extended, exploring health, foreign virus, motion sickness, foreign body, foreign DNA, bohemian lifestyle, gypsy life

4 HOUSE: Family health issue, growing family, homesick, family tree, house on the real estate market for an extended time, familial DNA, ancestors, family blood ties, domestic life

6 CLOUDS: Uncertainty surrounding a medical condition, mental health issue, hidden ailment, feeling under the weather, confusing ancestry, passing ailment, troubling health condition

7 SNAKE: Problems with health, bowel or digestive ailment, poisoned, kundalini, female healthcare worker, complicated ailment, twisted ankle

8 COFFIN: Major illness, end of life, shutting down of the body, fatal diagnosis, suppression of the immune system, drained life force, terminal illness, unhealthy, bad health

9 BOUQUET: Flourishing wellness, blooming health, cosmetic procedure, beautiful life, sweet nectar, essential oils, in the pink of health, flowers growing, wonderful growth, appreciating your ancestors, a wonderful life

10 SCYTHE: Sudden or unexpected illness, surgery required, injection (immunization), hazard to your health, scar, you reap what you sow, sorting out your life, broken bone, biopsy (growth removal)

11 WHIP: Muscle pain, questioning life, sports-related injury, rehabilitation, STD (sexually transmitted disease), questioning life, sexual dysfunction or impotence, sexual healing, sexual vigor

12 BIRDS: Gossiping about someone's health, conversation about health, sore throat, anxiety disorder, telehealth, talking about spirituality, nervous system

13 CHILD: Childhood illness, new health regiment, small health issue, the immune system, new growth, new life, minor illness

14 FOX: Manipulating the healthcare system, work life, misdiagnosis, undetected health issue, faking an illness, getting a second opinion, working overtime, defrauding the healthcare system

15 BEAR: Weight-related health issues, obesity, food allergies, eating disorder, large family tree, forced treatment (health), strong virus, a big tree

16 STARS: Wishing for better health, positive prognosis, electrical system, recovery, healthcare system, DNA strands, the astral body, positive life, aliened spiritually, the star system

17 STORK: Change in health, progressive health condition, changing your life, birth or a rebirth, pregnancy, changing health condition, evolving spiritually

18 DOG: Sense of smell affected, need to seek medical attention, therapy, therapy dog, friends for life, follow healthcare advice, protecting your health, friendship grows, familiar spiritual connection, support system

19 TOWER: Government healthcare system, hospital, clinic, past life, mandatory isolation (health), criminal-justice system, official diagnoses, well-established system, the backbone (spine)

20 GARDEN: Public health, group healing, public health concern, public life, earthing, forest, park, a garden grows, gathering in nature

21 MOUNTAIN: Setback in health, clogged body system, blockage-related illnesses, delayed recovery, sluggish health, blocked spiritual growth, distant or remote healing, impeded growth, hindered growth, stagnated growth, stubborn illness

22 PATHS: Multiple treatments, path to spirituality, alternative medicine, multiple lives, decision regarding health, alternative treatment, seeking a second opinion, possibilities begin to take root

23 MICE: Deteriorating, wasting away, sabotaging your life, feeling exhausted or depleted, stress-related illness, declining health, an epidemic, corrupt healthcare system, weakened immune system, a pandemic, widespread disease

24 HEART: Love grows, relationship health, initials on a tree, heart health, loving spiritual connection, loving life, in a relationship for a while

25 RING: Recurring health issue, circle of life, committed to a healthful lifestyle, married life, the circulatory system, continuing treatment

26 BOOK: Secret life, studying medicine, researching symptoms, student life, remembering an ancestor, secret spiritual connection, mysterious ailment, educational system

27 LETTER: Prescription, health certificate, doctor's note, results, letter regarding your health, sending healing vibes

28 MAN: Shaman, patient man, spiritual man, healthy man, male ancestor, physician, medicine man, male linage, natural man, virile man

29 WOMAN: Healer, patient woman, spiritual woman, healthy woman, female ancestor, physician, medicine woman, female linage, natural woman, fruitful woman

30 LILY: Age-related health problems, aging, arthritis, old illness, a lifetime, age slows you down, old life, air-conditioning system

31 SUN: Great health, recovery, sunburn, good health, successful life, willpower to heal, dehydration, sun care, vitamin D, sun therapy, solar system, heating system, thriving

32 MOON: Hormone-related health issues, practicing Reiki, lunacy, psychic healing, emotional health, intuitive life

33 KEY: Answers to a health inquiry, karmic life, noble bloodlines (DNA), significant growth, open to spending more time, importance placed on health, significant health concern

34 FISH: Hydration needed, water therapy, deeply rooted, financial health, alcoholism, serious health condition, financial life

35 ANCHOR: Stable growth, persistent illness, the pelvis, serious health concern, stuck for a while, long lasting and extended

36 CROSS: Suffering, pain, unable to heal, straining the health system, religious life, hindered growth, critical illness, enslaved to your health, burdened life

You know me; I think there ought to be a big old tree right there.
And let's give him a friend. Everybody needs a friend.
—Bob Ross

6 Clouds

Sad and confusing Clouds, pillows of light and dark
Obscure workings of the mind, the meaning so stark
Overcast and doubt, troubles swirling all around
Only by letting things go can a silver lining be found

KEYWORDS

Confusion, Sadness, Misunderstandings, Doubt, Uncertainty, Clouded judgment, Chaos, Vagueness, Bad weather, Insecurity, Despair, Depression, the Mind, Hidden, Fear, Troubles, Addictions, Obscured

MEANING

When Clouds shows up in your spread, remember that this too shall pass. The Cloud is a card of instability and obscurity denoting something is hidden, but not for long.

Lenormand Cloud Combinations

1 RIDER: Young man is putting on a front, news causes doubt, quick-moving storm, movement is erratic, news arriving is unclear, news is troubling, the Other Man is sad, suitor is confused, announcement is vague

2 CLOVER: Brief trouble, luck is uncertain, short-lived fear, gambling addiction, fleeting clouds, glimmer of happiness comes through

3 SHIP: Travel troubles, drifting about aimlessly, foreign unrest, moving through fear, exploring mental health, travel is doubtful at this time

4 HOUSE: Family dynamic is confusing, shelter from the rain, family chaos, family misunderstandings, house is dark, family member is sad, not sure about a house, a family member in hiding, family member feeling under the weather

5 TREE: Spiritually confused, medical cover-up, body dysmorphia, head in the clouds, health troubles, spiritual chaos, hiding a mental illness, growing unrest

7 SNAKE: Major misunderstanding, complications cause doubt, a snake pit, being led astray, toxic mind, lies create doubt, great problems, trouble brewing, desire is vague, lies cause confusion

8 COFFIN: Ending causes sadness, cause of death is unclear, ends with a misunderstanding, buried sadness, overwhelming grief, the end justifies the means, no fear, loss and grief, bad weather

9 BOUQUET: Irony, breakthrough, pretty moody, a wallflower, beautiful mind, pothead (marijuana), things are looking up, uplifted

10 SCYTHE: Sudden doubt, dangerously confused, cutting through the sadness, wreak havoc, irrevocable misunderstanding, dangerous doubt, separation causes confusion, clearing of the clouds, adrenaline junkie

11 WHIP: Arguments create uncertainty, OCD (obsessive compulsive disorder), sexual confusion, sex addict, tormenting depression, sexual misunderstanding, questioning your reality

12 BIRDS: Hearsay creates doubt, double trouble, anxious and scared, unrest, gossip creates trouble, unsettled weather, anxiety disorder

13 CHILD: Small misunderstanding, new doubts, play havoc with, small depression, major insecurity, a little sad, slight fear, a little bit of trouble

14 FOX: Pulling the wool over your eyes, employee misunderstanding, workaholic, job uncertainty, cleverly hidden, manipulation causes trouble, coworker causes trouble, under the cover of darkness, workplace turmoil

15 BEAR: Overbearing sadness, big doubt, huge misunderstanding, food addiction, boss has clouded judgment, feeding frenzy, formidable storm

16 STARS: Cloud storage, Creative Cloud, hope peeks though the clouds, clearing up doubt, clear mind, a silver lining, recognizing depression, clearing up confusion

17 STORK: Relocation causes doubt, the move is uncertain, long sadness, changing your mind, change is doubtful, progress is clouded, seasonal affective disorder (SAD), wishy-washy, postpartum depression

18 DOG: Loyalty is uncertain, help with mental illness, therapy, watch out for trouble, pay attention to mental health

19 TOWER: Mental health facility, rehab center, loneliness is hidden, company turmoil, isolation is confusing, past sorrow, isolation causes fear

20 GARDEN: Public uncertainty, mass confusion, public havoc, crowd frenzy, public mood, public fear, gathering your thoughts, social unrest

21 MOUNTAIN: Roadblock causes confusion, stubborn mind, setback causes sadness, landslide, obstacles cause doubt, lingering sadness

22 PATHS: Choice is unclear, decision brings sadness, procrastination, path is uncertain, decision causes doubt, choice is troubling

23 MICE: Worries cause fear, major doubt, someone is stealing your thunder, a mess, obsessive thoughts, lessening sadness, damaging thoughts

24 HEART: Love is uncertain, affection is misunderstood, relationship turmoil, a relationship is confusing, affection is hidden, relationship is judged

25 RING: Contract is unclear, agreement is confusing, marriage is doubtful, agreement is uncertain, continued trouble

26 BOOK: Education is uncertain, secrets are kept well hidden, remembering, research is inconclusive, research causes doubt, smoke and mirrors, information is obscured, secrets cause trouble

27 LETTER: Messages are vague, text message causes trouble, messages create doubt, documents are unclear, results are inconclusive

28 MAN: Confused man, sad man, moody man, troubled man, depressed man, unstable man, shady man, anarchist, man full of doubt, that man is trouble!

29 WOMAN: Confused lady, sad woman, moody woman, troubled lady, depressed woman, unstable woman, shady lady, rebellious woman, woman full of doubt, that woman is trouble!

30 LILY: Elderly person is confused (Alzheimer's disease), winter blues, retirement is unclear, peace of mind, retirement trouble, cold front

31 SUN: A silver lining, the conscious mind, a rainbow, here comes the sun, willpower, the sun shines through the clouds (illumination), things are getting better

32 MOON: Feeling confused, lunacy, moon madness, moon phases affect your mood, mood swings, feeling blue, feelings are vague, going through phases of doubt, feeling ungrounded, the subconscious mind, emotional turmoil

33 KEY: Revealing something hidden, karmic trouble, uncovering a mental illness, solution to your troubles, substantial doubts

34 FISH: Rain, black market, alcoholic, retail therapy, hidden spending, money troubles, shopping addiction (shopaholic)

35 ANCHOR: Lacking stability, having solid doubts, stubbornness, resistance is futile, heavy sadness, serious bad judgment, stuck in fear, long-lasting sadness

36 CROSS: Pain is confusing, major anguish, a holy terror, extreme sadness, terrible distress, a spirit is at unrest, extreme regret, vast sorrow, the struggle is real, paralyzed with fear, much remorse

Life's not about waiting for the storm to pass . . .
it's about learning to dance in the rain.
—Vivian Greene

7 Snake

Seductively alluring, an enemy lies in wait
When you see her coming, it's already too late
Betrayal and lies rest, on the tip of her forked tongue
Coiled and waiting, twisted problems are sprung

KEYWORDS

Complications, Seduction, Betrayal, Affairs, the Other Woman, Enemy, Desire, Toxic, Lies, Envy, Problems, Deception, Attraction, Transformation, Twisted, Jealousy, Issues, Temptation, Alluring, Wires & pipes

MEANING

When the shrewd Snake undulates its way into your reading, it is a warning for you to take pause. Look toward all the surrounding cards to see where the issue lies and how serious the problem will be. Traditionally representing the "Other Woman," this card carries a heavy connotation of lies and betrayal.

Lenormand Snake Combinations

1 RIDER: News is deceptive, announcement causes problems, suitor is lying, visitor causes problems, Other Man is jealous, quick seduction

2 CLOVER: Casual desire, lucky charm, game of seduction, gambling or gaming problems, charm bracelet, lucky twist, green with envy

3 SHIP: Journey is transformative, exploring desires, travel complications, tourist attraction, traveling to see another woman

4 HOUSE: Domestic problems, real estate complications, house envy, the house's pipes or plumbing, relative is untrustworthy, family problems

5 TREE: Health problems (possibly intestine or bowels), long-term affair with another woman, medical complication, spiritual transformation, growing lie, spiritual attraction, growing desire

6 CLOUDS: Hidden attraction, ominous threat, hidden desires, trouble is caused by another woman, hidden affair, hidden lies, concealing a problem, hidden enemy

8 COFFIN: Bad betrayal, buried desire, the cycle of life/death/rebirth, ending the affair with the Other Women, fatal attraction, bad lie, transformation, bad enemy, ending with a twist, death by poison, foreshadowing a problem, shedding your skin

9 BOUQUET: Attraction, appearances have been altered, flirting, gift for the Other Woman, blossoming attraction, show-off, surprise twist, appreciation for other women (roving eye), praising one's transformation, gift of a necklace or bracelet

10 SCYTHE: Surgical complication, irrevocable betrayal, sharp tongue, sudden attraction, burst pipes, cut wires, dangerous attraction, dangerous problem, broken dark-haired woman

11 WHIP: Sexual attraction, repeated betrayals, sexual desire, repetitive lies, raw sexual energy, striking out, sadism and masochism (S&M), sexually alluring, sexual problems, sex with the Other Woman, a pole dancer, a stripper, sexual issues, pattern of cheating

12 BIRDS: Talking with envy (forked tongue), tweeting lies, the couple deserves each other, talking seductively, gossiping about the Other Woman, nervous about lies told, unsettling problems

13 CHILD: Immature hurtful woman, easy target, new problem, immature desires, new enemy, small lie, small affair, small issue

14 FOX: Manipulating divorcee, work problems, manipulative liar, complication arises, clever seduction, sly betrayal, sneaking around with another woman, crafty manipulator, employee problems

15 BEAR: Powerful enemy, big problems, strong attraction, overbearing jealousy, great desire, food cravings, food issues, powerful temptation, large woman, formidable foe, big lie, major betrayal

16 STARS: Hoping for transformation, online attraction, Wi-Fi problems, exposing the lie, electrical wires, dreaming about another woman, electrical problems

17 STORK: The move is problematic, change brings transformation, baby fever, transforming (shedding your skin), returning issue, seasonal attraction

18 DOG: Loyalty is betrayed, frenemy, friend is lying, detecting a lie, you know the Other Woman (she's familiar to you), supporting another woman, receiving help with a transformation, watch out for complications

19 TOWER: Endless red tape, official complications, established affair, legal problems, telling tall lies, the law of attraction, very self-absorbed, official danger, kept woman, government lies

20 GARDEN: Public enemy, not as advertised, public attraction, meeting causes problems, public affair, group of women, meeting complications, public issue, public lies

21 MOUNTAIN: Insurmountable complications, stubborn woman, major trouble, delay causes problems, treacherous enemy, stubborn issue, being inflexible, clogged or blocked pipes

22 PATHS: Following your desire, choice is problematic, decision brings transformation, multiple affairs, unfamiliar woman

23 MICE: Declining desire, withering attraction, situation worsens, worried about problems, dirty lies, wearing down the enemy, degraded wires/pipes

24 HEART: Relationship envy, burning desire, relationship is twisted, love is betrayed, heart-related issues, relationship problems, heart's desire

25 RING: Surrounded by jealousy, ongoing affair, marital problems, surrounded by lies, deal is tempting, marital affair, circle of deceit, circulating lies

26 BOOK: Secrets and lies, a secret affair, a skeleton in the closet, secret desire, remembering an affair, a secret enemy, information is transformative

27 LETTER: Message causes problems, texting another woman, the message is deceptive, messages from another woman, results are complicated, communication issues, message of betrayal

28 MAN: Seductive man, dishonest man, cheating man, male enemy, toxic man, jealous man, charming man (snake charmer), deceptive man, mean man (mean like a snake), Prince Charming, snake oil salesman

29 WOMAN: Seductive female, dishonest woman, cheating female, female energy, toxic woman, jealous woman, striking lady, alluring woman, deceptive woman, mean woman, charlatan, sensual woman, the Other Woman, female enemy, curvy female

30 LILY: Old lie, old enemy, old affair, old plumbing, cold-blooded snake, old problem

31 SUN: Truth shines through, resolving problems, true enemy, courage after adversity, growth after a transformation, success after complications, easing of difficulties

32 MOON: Manifesting your desires, creative lies, an intuitive woman, an emotional affair, feeling betrayed, emotional problems, feeling desire

33 KEY: Karmic attraction, solving a problem, answers, revealing a desire, openly cheating, significant transformation, definite betrayal, uncovering a lie, explanation of a betrayal, uncovering a plot

34 FISH: Money problems, spending issues, financial lies, spending beyond your means, water pipes, cash flow issues, greed, business fraud, deep betrayal

35 ANCHOR: Entrenched with deception, long-standing lie, constant cheating, serious problems, long-lasting affair, going down the tubes, routine problems

36 CROSS: Burdened by problems, difficult betrayal, shameful lies, brutal enemy, horrific complications, victimized by the enemy, painful deception, burden of carrying the lies

*Just as a snake sheds its skin, we must shed our past
over and over again. —Jack Kornfield*

8 Coffin

Final goodbyes whispered softly, lives forever entwined
An echo of memories remain, sorrow for the ones left behind
Light gently touches the tomb, warming the weathered stone
That will one day be forgotten, buried by vines overgrown

KEYWORDS

Sorrow, Endings, Illness, Expired, Finality, Silence, Completion, Letting go, Dread, Grief, Loss, Emptiness, Mourning, Nothing, Death, Final outcome, No, Bad, Negativity, Buried, Stop, Closed, Nonexistent

MEANING

When the heavy Coffin appears, it brings with it a finality of sorts; you can be sure that something major in your life will be ending, causing a major shift and transformation.

Lenormand Coffin Combinations

1 RIDER: News of a passing, announcing an ending, news of an ending, announcing a death, moving through grief, sick young man, suitor ends it

2 CLOVER: Lucky ending, happy ending, easy passing, luck is fleeting, casual no, luck runs out, brief illness, minor sickness, game over

3 SHIP: Journey's end, transitioning in death, goodbye, trip is ending, moving toward completion, shipwreck, travel ban

4 HOUSE: House listing expires, family sorrow, comfort is ending, family in mourning, home is demolished, home is sold

5 TREE: Slow death, spiritual death, leaves falling, autumn, matter of life and death, deeply rooted grief, illness, diagnosis, growing sicker, drawn-out ending

6 CLOUDS: Confusing end, mental illness, major loss, depression, sadness and emptiness, indifference, in a cloud of grief, confusing illness, major grief, contemplating mortality, fear of dying

7 SNAKE: Complications resulting in death, flexible ending, major transition, seduction ends, toxic ending, transformation, complicated ending

9 BOUQUET: Memorial service, expressing yourself artistically, showing your art, pleasant ending, gift in a box, beautiful passing, surprising outcome, sweet release of death

10 SCYTHE: Sudden death, abrupt passing, struck down, abrupt silence, accidental death, unexpected death, quick death, cut your losses, major catastrophe, unexpected illness

11 WHIP: Conflict ends, orgasm (little death), sex ends, muscle loss, abuse ends, sex stops, questionable death, actively dying, competition ends

12 BIRDS: Couple calls it quits, gossip ceases, anxiety ends, a eulogy, conversation dies out, phone line is down, curiosity killed the cat

13 CHILD: Innocence ends, young life is lost, new beginning after an ending, alpha to omega, short illness, new ending, small silence

14 FOX: Employment loss, guilt results in emptiness, outsmarting death, manipulating the outcome, job ends, faking a death, an employee quits, suspicious death

15 BEAR: Leadership ends, power struggle stops, boss's death, diet ends, overbearing grief, big ending, grand finale, huge loss

16 STARS: Clear ending, there is hope at the end, finding relief at the end, hopeful outcome, a light shines in the dark, promising ending, relief at the end, wishing all ends well

17 STORK: Moving on and letting go, changes at the end, transitioning in death, changing the outcome, moving away for good, cycling through the stages of grief, pregnant silence

18 DOG: Friendship ends, a friend passes, supported through a loss, guarded silence, investigating a death, helping someone cross over

19 TOWER: Confinement, hospitalization, past needs to be released, official ending, official silence, formal mourning, ancient burial site, stubborn illness

20 GARDEN: Public memorial, a pandemic, public ending, public mourning, gathering for the last time, team loss, place is empty

21 MOUNTAIN: Obstacles at the end, stubborn silence, delays cause loss, delayed outcome, hard passing, impassive sadness, a hermit, stillness and silence of death, permanent affliction, hard passing

22 PATHS: Decision affects the outcome, path ends, separation causes emptiness, choice at the end, unusual ending, indecision causes death, alternative ending, road is empty, at the crossroads (journey of the dead)

23 MICE: Serious anxiety, very depleted, there is nothing left, fading away, obsessed with death, spoiled and expired, decomposing body, withering away to nothing, going . . . going . . . gone!

24 HEART: Relationship ends, love dies, love is gone, compassionate ending, heartache, lovesick, heartfelt passing, love is lost, love is empty

25 RING: Marriage is over, agreements are terminated, commitment ends, contracts expires, deal is lost, deal is final

26 BOOK: Education is completed, secrets are silenced, remembering the dead, Book of the Dead, a bookcase, mysterious death

27 LETTER: A will, certificate of death, obituary, correspondence ends, sending condolences, epilogue (writing an ending)

28 MAN: Negative man, grieving man, widow, empty man, unlucky man, bad man, dying man, closed-off man, deceased male, silent man, a dead man

29 WOMAN: Negative woman, grieving lady, widow, empty woman, unlucky lady, bad woman, dying woman, closed-off female, deceased female, silent woman

30 LILY: Peaceful passing, serene ending, discreet ending, old illness, expired, old grief, coldness ends

31 SUN: Successful ending, happy ending, improving illness, fortunate completion, light at the end of the tunnel, true death, meeting a courageous end, better-than-expected outcome, maybe, the Phoenix rises out of the ashes

32 MOON: Void of course (moon), creative block, necrophilia (fascination with death), feeling emotionally empty, mediumship, emotional void, feeling nothing

33 KEY: Fated ending, noble death, answers at last, karmic ending, relieved by letting go, answer is maybe, open casket, possibility emerges out of the ashes

34 FISH: Payments end, financial loss, money is gone, a safe (money box), watery grave, business closure, coffers are empty

35 ANCHOR: Stuck in a state of grief, long-lasting emptiness, weighed down by grief, inability to let go, keep holding on to an ending, routine outcome, serious illness, stuck and can't let go

36 CROSS: Painful outcome, critical ending, suicide, taxed to death, critical illness, victim until the end, self-sacrifice, being a martyr, burdened by silence, lesson learned at the end, suffering a loss, difficult death, Spirit crosses over

The smallest coffins are the heaviest.
—Ernest Hemingway

9 Bouquet

I sent you a bouquet of flowers, for one so dear
A heartfelt missive with a gift, wishing you were here
In appreciation of your beauty, so charming and fair
An invitation to love that will bloom everywhere

KEYWORDS

Invitation, Gift, Surprise, Beauty, Enjoyment, Charming, Flowers, Occasion, Sweet, Blossoming, Showy, Presentation, Design, Art, Color, Appreciation, Pleasant, Gratitude, Aesthetic, Fashion, Display, East

MEANING

As a card of beauty, when the Bouquet makes an appearance in a reading it is always a pleasant card to see. Influencing all the surrounding cards with its positive effect.

Lenormand Bouquet Combinations

1 RIDER: News is encouraging, encounter is wonderful, receiving an invitation, dancing, arriving from the East, receiving flowers, the visit is pleasant

2 CLOVER: Luck is blooming, temporary pleasure, lucky occasion, informal invitation, casual occasion, opportunity knocks, surprise invitation, clover the plant

3 SHIP: Departing gift, journey east, foreign beauty, trade show, exploring grat-

itude, travel invitation, farewell party, international fashion

4 HOUSE: House showing, home staging, "Home Sweet Home," family is thriving, home decor, home show, a house in the East, brand aesthetic, house-warming

5 TREE: Health is optimal, spirituality is blossoming, blooming, spiritual gratitude, health and wellness show, well-being, recovery, thriving, body sculpting, natural beauty

6 CLOUDS: Rain on your parade, obscure invitation, sad occasion, botched cosmetic procedure, dark art, storm is brewing in the East, hidden gem

7 SNAKE: Desiring beauty, manipulated by pleasantries, craving attention, the Other Woman is attractive, seduced by flattery, complicated design, alluring beauty

8 COFFIN: Ending of pleasantries, out of fashion, planting a seed, memorial flowers, end of happiness, final gift, turning down an invitation, dying flowers, preserving beauty, funeral

10 SCYTHE: Cut flowers, unexpected invitation, cutting out the pleasantries, shaving, surgical procedure (cosmetic)

11 WHIP: Sexual flattery, striptease, sex & candy, sexual gratification, repeated pleasure, sexual pleasure, erotic art, sexually gratifying

12 BIRDS: Conversation is pleasant, hectic occasion, oral presentation, verbal invitation, flying east, conversation is blooming, talking about fashion, discussing art, negotiations are pleasant

13 CHILD: Small gift, small token of appreciation, birthday party, small presentation, birthday gift, small pleasure, first date, little gratitude, youthful beauty

14 FOX: Employee appreciation, con artist, suspicious invite, false flattery, superficial beauty, work presentation, job in the East, work invitation, manipulating beauty, guilt gift, work surprise, job in interior design, taking advantage of a gift, fake beauty, guilty pleasure

15 BEAR: An influencer, overbearing generosity, powerful art, sweets & candy, imposing invitation, big gift, bold colors, large display, huge appreciation, big bouquet of flowers, big presentation

16 STARS: Dreams are blossoming, hope is blooming, highest recognition, tech presentation, digital art, encouraging request, stargazing, inspirational art, positive occasion, stunning beauty, northeast

17 STORK: Change is beautiful, the move is pleasant, redesigning, baby shower invitation, moving east, returning a gift, baby shower gift, baby shower, exchanging gifts, changing your appearance, spring, spring flowers

18 DOG: Friendly occasion, friendly appreciation, unconditional gratitude, dog show, friendly invite, helpful gift

19 TOWER: Formal invitation, official thank-you, past occasion, formal presentation, tower in the East, grand design, conceited (beauty), traditional gift

20 GARDEN: Public occasion, team gratitude, meeting presentation, public display, exhibition, social invite, public presentation, open invitation, popular fashion, group invitation, garden show, wild flowers

21 MOUNTAIN: Holding back enjoyment, rustic decor, delayed invitation, blocking pleasure, permanent makeup, tattoo, challenging design, mountain in the East

22 PATHS: Choice is presented, choosing a gift, deciding whom to invite, walking eastward, alternative artist, choosing gratitude, choosing colors, many presents, choose the path east, decisions about cosmetic surgery, choosing flowers

23 MICE: Spoiling something nice, dried flowers, stolen gift, diminished pleasure, fading beauty, declining an invitation, ruining an occasion, stolen gift

24 HEART: Romance is budding, heartfelt invitation, love is blossoming, heart-shaped face, kind gesture, heart full of gratitude, loving gift, heartfelt appreciation, generosity, romantic gift, love poem

25 RING: Agreement is satisfying, wedding invitation, deal is favorable, round face, wedding flowers, marriage proposal, continual gratitude

26 BOOK: Secret admirer, secret gift, studying herbalism, researching art, graduating with distinction or honors, secret appreciation, studying art, information is pleasant, book fair

27 LETTER: An invitation, a letter of appreciation, writing poetry, letter of congratulations, message of admiration, sending flowers, a written presentation

28 MAN: Social man, handsome man, conceited man, delightful man, wonderful man, considerate man, artist, flashy man, grateful man, sweet man, pleasant man, poetic man, polite man

29 WOMAN: Social butterfly, beautiful woman, fashionable woman, artist, conceited woman, delightful woman, wonderful lady, considerate woman, fancy female, grateful lady, sweet woman, pleasant female, poetic female, polite woman

30 LILY: Peaceful occasion, retirement gift, private occasion, lilies, old invitation, pure appreciation, aging gracefully, cultivated flower

31 SUN: Sunrise, happy occasion, cheerfulness, happiness, warm compliments, warm gratitude, happy celebration, a sunflower, holiday decorations, true beauty, southeast

32 MOON: Creative presentation, a moonflower, intuitive gifts, a moon face, creative art, creative decor, feeling beautiful, intuitive art

33 KEY: Important occasion, important presentation, solution is presented, opening ceremonies, open invitation, fine art, opening a gift

34 FISH: Monetary gift, deep gratitude, business surprise, purchasing art, money spent on beauty products, shopping for a gift, business presentation, company appreciation, corporate gifts, financial presentation

35 ANCHOR: Lasting gratitude, coastal colors, beach house decor, solid presentation, safe presentation

36 CROSS: Obligatory gift, unhappy occasion, devotional art, burdened by an invitation, cruel surprise, tough occasion, religious occasion, religious gift

Always keep that happy attitude.
Pretend that you are holding a beautiful fragrant bouquet.
—Earl Nightingale

10 Scythe

The arc of the blade cutting with extreme precision
Accidents and reckonings abruptly cause a great division
A dangerous severing of ties, and many broken things,
These are the unexpected wounds that the Scythe brings

KEYWORDS

Sudden, Irrevocable, Accident, Sever, Remove, Reap, Divide, Gather, Cut, Harvest, Reckoning collect, Surgery, Wound, Danger, Rupture, Unexpected, Clears a path, West, Reckoning, Broken, Disconnected, Separate, Detached, Risk, Autumn

MEANING

The Scythe a dangerous card, always coming in suddenly, without warning, when you least expect it. It can clear a path, removing anything that stands in its way, but can also cut and wound with equal vigor. Look to the surrounding cards to see what the Scythe is up to.

Lenormand Scythe Combinations

1 RIDER: News about an accident, visit is cut short, quick accident, very quickly, arrival of danger, young man is impulsive, announcing a separation

2 CLOVER: Brief breakup, opportunity missed, small gain collected, luck is unexpected, lucky break, happiness is unexpected

3 SHIP: Journey west, car accident, travel-related injury, distance is permanent, trip cut short, movement is cut off

4 HOUSE: Property damage, house taken off the market, brand suicide, real estate risk, family ties severed, lease agreement is terminated, family disconnected, family member is in danger, a home divided

5 TREE: Surgery, deeply rooted scars, breaking a bone, a spiritual wound, dental procedure, spiritually disconnected, organ rupture, wounded

6 CLOUDS: Clouds gathering, misunderstandings are irrevocable, mental breakdown, hiding a breakup, lost and disconnected, mentally detached, hidden danger, concealed weapon, confusing separation

7 SNAKE: Complicated separation, pipes rupture, desire ends suddenly, wires are cut, sudden and unexpected, lies cause damage, complicated surgery

8 COFFIN: Ending is final, ending suddenly, fatal accident, burying the hatchet, final outcome, no surgery, silent and detached, death is certain, the end, final blow, the ends justify the means, no vaccine, grave danger, empty threats, the Grim Reaper

9 BOUQUET: Haircut, cosmetic surgery, pleasant surprise, civilized separation, surprise break, invitation was unexpected, tattoo removal, beautiful gathering, art collection, east–west

11 WHIP: Conflict was wounding, aggressively cutting, pattern of violence, taking a sexual break, physical removal, exercise injury, a quickie (sex), sexual violence

12 BIRDS: Arguments, slander, speaking impulsively, a couple separates, nervous breakdown, talks about separation, conversation causes damage, negotiations are cut off

13 CHILD: Growth spurt, childhood injury, newly separated, little break, small surgery, new danger, small wound, simple surgery, little dangerous

14 FOX: Job cuts, work hours slashed, job share, work break, scammed, superficial wound, workplace accident or injury, outsmarting danger, occupational hazard, manipulation is damaging

15 BEAR: Caloric reduction (a diet), big break, powerful reckoning, more than expected, slow things down, big accident, huge risk, big danger

16 STARS: Positive separation, hope is gathering, dreams are impulsive, reputation is damaged, famous all of a sudden, positive removal, exposing the danger, northwest

17 STORK: Leg injury, change happens without warning, recurring break, progress is cut off, moving suddenly, seasonal damage, moving out west, moving away from danger, the move is risky, spring break

18 DOG: A friend is broken, trust is broken, help is denied, loyalty is damaged, remaining friends after a breakup, amicable separation, "I smell danger," friend is cut off, warning of danger, investigating an accident

19 TOWER: Hospital operating room, emergency room, legal judgment is irrevocable, official separation, pride causes damage, adding insult to injury, officially in danger

20 GARDEN: Gathering unexpectedly, social suicide, a team divided, breakout (meeting), community danger, social gathering, meeting is cut short, public gathering, collecting and gathering, meeting unexpectedly

21 MOUNTAIN: A hard separation, permanent removal, limits removed, restrictions are lifted, blocking danger, uphill battle

22 PATHS: Decision is sudden, elective surgery, leading to danger, the choice is unexpected, path is dangerous, the choice is irrevocable, unusual accident

23 MICE: Decaying bounty, deteriorating rapidly, less than expected, costly accident, depleting quickly, gnawing danger, a dirty wound, messy separation

24 HEART: Love hurts, love cut off, heartbreak, heart surgery, love divided, flirting with danger, relationship is abruptly cut off

25 RING: Contract is irrevocable, commitment is severed, divorce, breakup, vows are broken

26 BOOK: Unknown danger, education cut off, research is collected, memories are removed, reading break, knowledge can be dangerous

27 LETTER: Communication is cut off, message is cutting, message sent accidentally, text message, messages removed

28 MAN: Impulsive man, hurtful man, an ex, ruthless man, dangerous man, decisive man, broken man, cutting off a man, severing ties with a man, divorced man

29 WOMAN: Impulsive lady, hurtful woman, an ex, ruthless woman, dangerous female, decisive female, broken woman, cutting off a woman, severing ties with a female, divorced woman

30 LILY: Old wounds, late harvest, peace is broken, retired unexpectedly, old married couple splits up, winter break

31 SUN: A successful harvest, reaping the rewards, a courageous separation, a welcome release, the truth is unexpected, a happy accident, southwest, summer break

32 MOON: Manifests suddenly, recognized immediately, influence is removed, creative breakthrough, feeling detached, emotionally cut off, emotionally detached, psychic wounds

33 KEY: Karma is certain, significant separation, access is suddenly granted, opened accidentally (Pandora's box), revealing danger, open wound, important division, celebrated harvest

34 FISH: Money flows unexpectedly, wage cut, wealth cut off, financially cut off, price cut, drinking dangerously, earnings cut, commissions slashed, deep cuts, cost cutting, assets divided

35 ANCHOR: Heavy damage, serious danger, routine surgery, serious break, settling down abruptly, long-lasting wounds, routine separation

36 CROSS: Obligations are piling up, a reckoning, burdens are gathering, sorrows cut deeply, suffering will be experienced, a painful wound, suffering cuts deeply, painful break, spirit removal, exorcist

Life is like a field,
where we must gather what we grow, weed, or wheat . . .
this is the law, we reap the crop we sow.
—Patience Strong

11 Whip

Feeding the empty darkness, biting deep within me
Accepting the abuse, as sex keeps setting me free
Arguments so violent, wax drips as the pleasure grows
Marks left on my body, borne witness by the crows

KEYWORDS

Aggression, Arguments, Sex, Assault, Abuse, Disputes, Active, Patterns, Hit, Violence, Debate, Exercise, Discipline, Repetitive, Anger, Strike, Disruptive, Conflict, Punishment, Criticize, Opposition, Habit, Interruption, Competition, Attack, Questions

MEANING

The Whip brings a heightened sexual energy, and when it appears, it brings an intensity to everything it lashes out at and touches. This card is indicative of something repetitive and recurring, bringing an element of noise and disruption into your life.

Lenormand Whip Combinations

1 RIDER: News of violence, impending punishment, athletic activity, news is repetitive, a quickie (sex), visitor is abusive, quick to anger

2 CLOVER: Fleeting conflict, gambling habit, informal questioning, gambling competition, casual sex, lucky strike, brief struggle, exiting sex life, spontaneous sex, keep trying, gambling (taking a chance repeatedly)

3 SHIP: Trip interruption, traveling repeatedly, traveling to have sex, adventurous sex, exploring sexuality, foreign violence, international threat

4 HOUSE: Domestic violence, family squabbles, real estate bidding war, house is relisted, family arguments, house of ill repute, an active home, real estate questions

5 TREE: Deeply rooted conflict, health questions, healthful competition, healthful habits, growth is interrupted, past abuse, healthful exercise, healthful dose of anger, healing abuse, growth comes from conflict, tantric sex

6 CLOUDS: Hidden abuse, confusing argument, mood swings, concealed violence, lightning strikes, hiding sexual activity, mindfucking, storm activity, obscure questions, hidden threat

7 SNAKE: Enemy assault, lying repeatedly, cheating in a competition, toxic habit, desiring punishment, BDSM (bondage, discipline, domination, submission, sadism, masochism), need to exercise, cheating physically, belly dancing, the Other Woman just won't go away, kinky sex, betrayed sexually, the enemy strikes!

8 COFFIN: End of conflict, no sex, buried abuse, final question, ending sexual relations, losing the argument, an autopsy, bad sex, sick of having sex, bad habit, stop arguing!

9 BOUQUET: Voyeurism, enjoying sex, design competition, blossoming sex life, sweet sting of pain, pleasurable activity, face yoga, invitation to have sex, beauty routine, design patterns, art competition, the art of persuasion, beauty or art critic.

10 SCYTHE: Sudden argument, aggravated assault, dangerous questions, severe punishment, adding injury to insult, wounding abuse, cutting off sex, dangerous habit, unexpected disputes, dangerously abusive, unexpected aggression, dangerous competition, immediate retribution, dangerous assault, dangerous pattern, breaking a habit

12 BIRDS: Gossiping vigorously, oral sex, verbal abuse, music critic, phone sex, sibling squabbles, nervous sexual energy, talking about sex, singing competition, asking questions

13 CHILD: Small argument, new threat, playful sex, new pattern, innocent questions, new habit, child abuse, bullying, little bit competitive, little bit aggressive, childish dispute, underage sex

14 FOX: Sneaking around for sex, manipulating someone into sex, on-the-job training, sneaky competitor, tricky questions, cunningly aggressive, illegal activity, fraudulent competition, job interview, workplace dispute, outsmarting the competition

15 BEAR: Powerful aggression, diet and exercise, big question, very aggressive, a dominant, bodybuilder, big competition, bear attack, body sculpting, huge argument, large disruption, food critic

16 STARS: Wishing repeatedly, online sex, hoping for sex, clearing conflict, online questions, exposing abuse, starstruck, movie critic, highly disciplined, keyboard warrior (online debates)

17 STORK: Change causes arguments, seasonal activities, moving back and forth, switching, recurring abuse, springtime activities

18 DOG: Animal abuse, friends with benefits, investigation questions, dog competition, a submissive, friendly competition, dog training, dog attack, dogfight, dog bite

19 TOWER: Government rhetoric, legal debate, a penis (manhood), an erection, legal punishment, the gym, a prison, a strip club, stiff penalty, legal dispute, the opposition, capital punishment, formal questioning

20 GARDEN: Public display of affection (PDA), public competition, meeting questions, public humiliation, group sex, team competition, public argument, pubic threat

21 MOUNTAIN: Obstacle course, hard questions, permanent grudge, hard workout, insurmountable conflict, challenging argument, rough sex, harshly criticized, mountain climbing

22 PATHS: Multiple sex partners, decision causes arguments, unusual questions, multiple competitions, many questions, on a road to conflict, planning to have sex, alternative sexuality

23 MICE: Dwindling sex drive, dirty sex, stressful interview, less competition, draining argument, less active, obsessive questioning, diminished anger, damaging abuse, dirty habits, damaging criticism

24 HEART: Passionate sex, heart attack, relationship patterns, love is a battlefield, relationship questions, dating competition, affectionate banter, lovemaking, lovers' spat, generous lover

25 RING: Going around and around in circles, contract violation, bondage, continual abuse, marriage conflict, handcuffs, continued punishment, circular pattern, marital spat

26 BOOK: Secretly fighting, having secret sex, studying, secret competition, researching sex, secret habit, there is a history of abuse, history repeats itself, book critic

27 LETTER: Written permission, written threats, message causes conflict, scheduled sex, writing competition, messages are repetitive, texts messages sent back and forth

28 MAN: Aggressive man, argumentative man, abusive man, sexual man, a dominant, violent man, kinky man, abused man, creature of habit, active man, sexy man, competitive man, personal trainer

29 WOMAN: Aggressive woman, argumentative lady, abusive woman, sexual female, feisty female, kinky female, abused woman, creature of habit, fierce woman, active female, sexy lady, a dominatrix, competitive female, personal trainer

30 LILY: Discreet sex, old conflicts, old habits, passive aggressive, marital sex, old abuse, private competition, senior exercise, winter activities, elder abuse

31 SUN: Winning the argument, good sex, healing from abuse, good habits, easy workout, heated competition, summer activities, growth from conflict, energy surge

32 MOON: Emotional abuse, creative sex life, nightly exercise, psychic attack, creative competition, fantasizing about sex, feeling sexy, moonstruck, intuitive hit, skilled debater

33 KEY: Open competition, promiscuous, resolving an argument, important questions, free from abuse, revealing argument, answer to violence, solution to conflict, openly critical

34 FISH: Financial transactions, overspending repeatedly, buying sexual favors, spending habits, financial questions, banking activity, financial competition, alcohol abuse, a hookup, luring someone into sex

35 ANCHOR: Safe sex, long-lasting conflict, vanilla sex, serious persuasion, routine questions, lingering argument, safe competition, unchanged habit, weight lifting, protective sex (condoms)

36 CROSS: Necessary conflict, vital argument, disappointing sex, test questions, spirit activity, shameful habit, essential exercise, celibacy, painful abuse, punishment

> *Sticks and stones may break my bones,*
> *but chains and whips excite me.*
> *—Rihanna*

12 Birds

Chattering, tweeting, and gossiping about everybody's life
Conversations, and negotiations, curiosity causes strife
Nervous and anxiously flitting, over here and over there
Fragile wind-borne nesters, always appearing in a pair

KEYWORDS

Verbal, Conversations, Chatter, Restlessness, Nervousness, Anxiety, Gossip, Music, Noisy, a Pair, a Couple, Talkative, Vocal, Excited, Hectic, Whispers, Negotiations, Phone calls, Curious, Spoken words, Rumors

MEANING

The Birds card is bustling and full of hectic, anxious energy and always has something to say, rushing off with something to do. The Birds always represent the spoken word, indicative of a pair or two of something.

Lenormand Bird Combinations

1 RIDER: News broadcast, news is exciting, cadence of speech, news is widespread, quick phone call, visitor is a busybody, guest is restless, quick conversation, fast talker

2 CLOVER: Casual phone call, brief excitement, carefree words, informal meeting, casual conversation, fleeting gossip, easy conversation, small opportunity to talk, casual conversation, whistling, a lucky pair

3 SHIP: Foreign language, airplane, traveling to a concert, a flight, pirated music, traveling by plane, foreign couple, long-distance phone call

4 HOUSE: Real estate negotiations, flatmates, roommates, nesting, a nest, siblings, family gossip, family discussions, house music

5 TREE: Lengthy conversations, deeply rooted anxiety, extended negotiations, healing conversations, sore throat, extended negotiations, spiritual talks

6 CLOUDS: Hidden conversation, major anxiety, nervousness, cacophony, turbulence, confusing conversation, the blues (music), troubling gossip, discord, sad phone call

7 SNAKE: Jealous rumors, toxic conversation, complicated negotiation, venomous gossip, a rumor, a forked tongue, dishonest conversation

8 COFFIN: Concluding talks, ending a call, don't speak, ending negotiations, silent partner, silence, death metal (music), end of conversation, shut your mouth, silencing rumors, final conversation, closed negotiations, stop talking!

9 BOUQUET: Fashion talks, flowery words, poetry, beautiful couple, flattering words spoken, sweet talk, surprising conversation, charming conversation

10 SCYTHE: Risky negotiations, disconnected couple, cutting off talks, damaging conversation, sharp words spoken, separation anxiety, cutting remarks, cutting off communications, dangerous couple

11 WHIP: Sexual conversation, performance anxiety, sexually excited, booty call, sexual rumors, repetitive conversations, abusive conversation, sexual tension, sexual curiosity

13 CHILD: Small rumor, new gossip, short negotiations, making small talk, vulnerable conversation, slight anxiety, playful banter, siblings, beginning negotiations, immature conversation, new couple, a little bit anxious

14 FOX: Tricky negotiations, workplace gossip, superficial conversation, job anxiety, guilty of gossiping, misleading conversation, clever words, suspicious conversation, manipulative conversation, a scheming couple

15 BEAR: Overbearing couple, big negotiations, powerful rumor, forced conversation, diet causes anxiety, powerful gossip, a power couple, strong words spoken

16 STARS: Social media, Twitter feed, influential couple, cell phone, hopeful negotiations, meaningful conversation, inspirational talks, stirring song, celebrity gossip ("spilling the tea"), harmonious music, positive discussion, a famous couple, online chat

17 STORK: Bustling nervous energy, long conversation, translating, pregnant with twins, pregnancy rumors, baby talk, relocation rumors, very restless, migration

18 DOG: Friendly conversation, a loyal couple, familiar chatter, supportive talks, supportive partner, chewing someone out, friendly couple, naturally curious, friendly negotiation, investigating a rumor, watch out for gossip!

19 TOWER· Official word, legal negotiations, official talks, arrogant conversation, jailbird, established couple, formal discussion, past conversations, recanting a statement

20 GARDEN: Everyone is gossiping, public excitement, public negotiations, country music, social anxiety, public unrest, group chat (social media), public conversation, choir, concert, group discussions

21 MOUNTAIN: Delayed flight, hard conversation, stubborn couple, rock music, challenging negotiation, agitation, harsh words spoken, putting off a conversation, difficult conversation, persistent anxiety

22 PATHS: Decision causes anxiety, multiple conversations, alternative couple, unusual conversation, choice words, many phone calls

23 MICE: Costly rumors, damaging gossip, fears cause anxiety, dirty words, losing your voice, group gossip, gnawing nervousness, worrisome conversation, nagging curiosity, opportunistic chatter, obsessed with music

24 HEART: Romantic couple, loving conversation, passionate about music, relationship gossip, heart flutters (butterflies), whispering sweet nothings, lovebirds, passionate conversation, love song, relationship rumors

25 RING: Committed couple, contract negotiations, wedding bands, connecting flight, put your records on, commitment anxiety, marriage rumors, contained gossip (to a small circle), circulating gossip, wedding song, married couple, wedding jitters

26 BOOK: Secret negotiations, whispers, educational discussions, secret conversations, informative talks, intelligent conversation

27 LETTER: Transcript, text message, email, tweet, writing songs, Snapchat, DM (direct message), any electronic conversation

28 MAN: Talkative man, nervous man, restless man, vocal man, curious male, male singer, male musician, pilot, flight attendant, gossiping man, brother, anxious man, two men, same-sex couple

29 WOMAN: A bird, "Chatty Cathy," nervous lady, restless woman, vocal lady, curious female, female singer, female musician, pilot, flight attendant, gossiping woman, sister, anxious woman, two ladies, same-sex couple

30 LILY: Snowbirds, two old men, older couple, private negotiations, old rumor, stale gossip, cold conversation, mature discussion, private conversation

31 SUN: Successful negotiations, courageous conversation, warm couple, real conversation, fortunate discussion, good talk, relief from anxiety, joy, daily gossip, good communicator, optimistic conversation, there's some truth to a rumor

32 MOON: Creative negotiations, intuitive conversation, nightly talks, fortune-telling, emotional anxiety, feeling restless, meditation music, pillow talk

33 KEY: Open negotiations, significant conversation, free bird, distinguished couple, open to talking, a password, revealing gossip, keynote speech, uncovering rumors, open mic, fated couple, freedom song, answer the phone, openly gossiping

34 FISH: Money talks, business negotiations, business partner, flowing conversation, deep discussion, financial discussions, financial negotiations

35 ANCHOR: Serious conversation, steady partnership, heavy conversation, a seagull, constant anxiety, long-lasting negotiations, stable couple, safe discussion, heavy metal (music)

36 CROSS: Tough negotiations, disappointing conversation, painful words are spoken, religious discussions, devotional songs, religious chant, hymns, shameful gossip, a sermon, exhausting conversation, victim of gossip, a religious couple, painful conversation, obligated communication

A flock of flirting flamingos is pure, passionate, pink pandemonium—
a frenetic flamingle-mangle—a discordant discotheque of delirious
dancing, flamboyant feathers, and flamingo lingo.
—Charley Harper

13 Child

Playful dear little Child, full of wonder, young and new
Sweet and innocent you are, before my eyes you grew
Hold on tightly to the magic for as long as you can
Because soon the thief of time will turn this boy into a man

KEYWORDS

New, Simple, Playful, Small things, Little, Naive, Wonder, Beginning, Trusting, Vulnerable, Inexperience, Innocent, Fresh start, Immature, Timid, Childhood, Short, Insecure, Slight

MEANING

The Child card brings an aura of innocence and a touch of naivety to any situation of inquiry. When asking about an issue the Child card refers to something little or small, or even a child.

Lenormand Child Combinations

1 RIDER: Young boy, first-time visitor, delivery of a small package, the first child, visit from a child, comings and goings of a child (shared custody)

2 CLOVER: Lucky start, carefree child, the game begins, chance for a new beginning, happy childhood, game play, opportunity for a fresh start, cheerful child

3 SHIP: Foreign child, school bus, exploring something new, saying farewell to a child, moving toward a fresh start

4 HOUSE: A family with children, daycare, nursery, the family is vulnerable, real estate novice, brand new, a family member is vulnerable

5 TREE: Growing child, life interrupted, growth, DNA test, healthful start, the illness is minor, spiritual growth, a growing insecurity, major growth, turning over a new leaf

6 CLOUDS: Insecurity, depressed youth, a sad child, obscure beginnings, misunderstood youth, puzzling first step, lost youth, confused child, fearful child, vague start, hide and seek

7 SNAKE: Complicated child, problem child, selfish child, pipes / electric wires are fragile, twisted beginning, difficult child, desires are immature, lying child

8 COFFIN: End of innocence, the last child, death of a child, no children, mourning a child, ill child, bad start, the end of the beginning, bad childhood, letting go of a child, no steps taken

9 BOUQUET: Attractive child, enjoying childhood, sweet child, grateful for a new beginning, invitation to a children's party, charming child, gift of toys, design is simple, thankful for a fresh start

10 SCYTHE: Suddenly vulnerable, disconnected child, injured child, dangerous start, dangerous play, removing a child

11 WHIP: Sexually inexperienced, competitive child, punishing a child, questioning a child, hyperactive child, scolding a child, sexually immature, sex toys, sexually vulnerable, threatening a child, sexually timid, striking a child, criticizing a child

12 BIRDS: Two children, nervous child, lullaby, talkative child, anticipating a fresh start, siblings, negotiations are straightforward, eager to begin something new, a couple with children

14 FOX: Sneaky child, guilty child, a nanny, surviving childhood, clever child, work shortage, job inexperience, working a little, manipulating an innocent, scheming child, false start, working with children, running a game, exploiting a child

15 BEAR: Powerful start, empowering a child, big bully, chubby child, mother or grandmother of the child, forceful play

16 STARS: Hoping for a fresh start, inspirational new beginning, Starseed (Star-Child), famous child, clear beginning, bright child, positive fresh start

17 STORK: New beginning, birth of a child, skinny child, restless child, pregnancy, the move is simple, moving for a fresh start, springtime brings a fresh start

18 DOG: A puppy, friendly child, trusting child, loyal child, protecting a child, friend's child

19 TOWER: Aloof teen, a school, a teenager, withdrawn teen, a tall child, a hospital for sick children, growing up, lonely child, official start, juvenile detention, custody regarding a child, stubborn child, verdict is innocent

20 GARDEN: A playground, amusement park, playdate, social child, a park, "It takes a village to raise a child," socially inexperienced, meeting someone new

21 MOUNTAIN: Challenging child, delayed start, stubborn child, distant child, difficult child, impeded growth, a hard start

22 PATHS: Unusual start, multiple children, choice is simple, unfamiliar child, planning a new beginning, possibly innocent, path leading to a fresh start

23 MICE: Stressful beginning, damaged child, costly childhood, nagging child, spoiled brat, robbed of a fresh start, lost boys

24 HEART: Caring child, love is naive, beloved child, relationship is short lived, compassionate child, loving child, passionate new beginning, pleasurable childhood, a love child

25 RING: Adoption, contract is simple, connection is vulnerable, married with children, continually starting over, married for a short time, continuously growing

26 BOOK: Unknown vulnerability, mysterious childhood, learning new knowledge, secret child, smart kid, masking vulnerability, secretive child, student, brilliant child

27 LETTER: Communication begins, email shows vulnerability, messages are playful, results are simple, mailing out small things

28 MAN: Young man, vulnerable man, immature man, new man, small man, innocent man, short man, naive man, man-child, playful man, inexperienced man, slight man, a boy

29 WOMAN: Young lady, vulnerable woman, immature woman, new woman, petite lady, innocent woman, short woman, naive lady, playful woman, inexperienced female, timid woman, slight woman, a girl

30 LILY: Grandchild, father or grandfather of the child, peaceful beginning, old soul, midlife, eldest child, retiring early, certain innocence, older child

31 SUN: Successful start, joyful childhood, vital fresh start, male child, thriving child, courageous child, fresh burst of willpower, good first step, sunny new beginning, truth is simple, optimistic beginning

32 MOON: Intuitive child, inner child, creative new beginning, manifesting a fresh start, female child, psychic child, emotionally immature, feeling vulnerable, emotional child, feeling insecure

33 KEY: Very open, important first step, destined child, significant beginning, answer is simple, access is short, revealing insecurity, showing vulnerability, an open child

34 FISH: Financially insecure, business inexperience, the flow of new money, sugar baby, business is vulnerable, putting money first

35 ANCHOR: Serious child, reliable child, steady start, a routine start, a safe start, stuck in immaturity, safety first

36 CROSS: Painful childhood, abandoned child, tough start, difficult child, remorseful, child, obligated first step, burdened child, religious vulnerability

A child is an uncut diamond.
—Austin O'Malley

14 Fox

Peering into the depths of your soul, an icy cold stare
Approach me very cautiously and challenge me if you dare
Work your instincts wisely, manipulation is what I teach
Once you understand this, nothing will ever be out of reach

KEYWORDS

Cunning, Work, Clever, Sly, Trickery, Instinct, Survival, Manipulation, Fraudulent, Predatory, Outsmart, Untrustworthy, Elude, Stealth, Scam, Witty, Guilty, False, Fake, Suspicion, Caution, Mistake, Con, Superficial

MEANING

The sly Fox is very cunning and will do whatever it takes to make sure that he always comes out on top. As long as his family is safe and provided for, the Fox will never shy away from work.

Lenormand Fox Combinations

1 RIDER: News of employment, news about a coworker, coming and going from job to job, postal worker, getting a delivery at work, commuting to work, suitor at work, journalist, delivery person, beware a visitor is untrustworthy!

2 CLOVER: Temporary employment, promotion, temporary gig, lucky break at work, casual job, informal job interview, lucky instinct, small opportunity at work, easy work, fun job, happy workplace, casino employee, short-term job

3 SHIP: Traveling for work, travel agent, foreign employee, overseas job, leaving a job, travel advisory, travel scam, a driver

4 HOUSE: Domestic worker, homework, housework, a family member is acting suspicious, indoor job, homemaker, real estate scam, branding mistake, inside job

5 TREE: Healthcare worker, health sciences, health and safety at work, misdiagnosis, health scam, healthcare fraud, spiritual hocus-pocus, deeply rooted suspicion

6 CLOUDS: Smoke and mirrors, hidden scam, turmoil at work, dark scheme, shadow work, sad coworker, mental health worker, trouble brewing, doubting an employee, fear of job loss, hidden agenda, uncertain job situation, confusing job, upset employee

7 SNAKE: Lies and betrayal, venomous threat, illegal behaviors, perilous situation, unsafe actions, lying employee, enemy at work, toxic workplace, extremely untrustworthy, predatory, problematic employee, attracted to a coworker, snake oil salesman

8 COFFIN: Unemployment, negative outcome, loss of employment, no job, a mortician, a medium, a necromancer, buried guilt, death fraud, termination of employment, negative coworker, buried in work, dead-end job, quitting a job

9 BOUQUET: Pleasant job, attractive job offer, a beautician, a hairstylist, an artist, a designer, grateful for work, gift given to manipulate, an occasion a work (a work thing), pleasant work atmosphere

10 SCYTHE: Job resignation, layoff, redundancy, risky job, accident at work, dangerous employee, cutting jobs, unexpected fraud, dangerous scam

11 WHIP: Demanding job, abusive manipulation, critical employee, sex scam, training at work, coaching, a personal trainer, a dominatrix, sexual manipulation, sexual instinct, sex work, questionable work, sexual guilt, physical job, competing for a job

12 BIRDS: Conversation at work, interview, unorganized workplace, a singer, a musician, rumors about an employee, talking shop, two-faced, talking behind your back, stressful workplace, music gig, gossip at work

13 CHILD: New employee, child labor, small job, small scam, child exploitation, playing a trick, inexperienced employee, vulnerable to a scam, new job

15 BEAR: Powerful instinct, overbearing manager, big scam, big job, aggressive coworker, huge workload, forced labor, powerful job

16 STARS: Promotion, star employee, technical job, internet scam, a PR agent (public relations), online job, social-media influencer, online scam, online manipulation, online gig

17 STORK: Changing your job, relocating for work, seasonal work, reworking something, migrant worker, shift work, returning to work, evolving job role, seasonal job

18 DOG: Reliable employment, loyal employee, dog trainer, investigating an employee, a detective, a support worker, friendly colleagues, exhibiting pack behavior at work, a police officer, amicable workplace, dependable work, help wanted, trust your instinct!

19 TOWER: Corporate manipulation, MLM (multilevel marketing) scam, human resources, a politician, government employee, established career, past employment, a civil servant, government agenda, up to no good!, government fraud, verdict is guilty!

20 GARDEN: Stalker, teamwork, social-media scam, led down the garden path, general meeting at work, outdoor job, public scandal, community meeting, a gardener, a social worker, group work, socializing with an agenda, general labor, social networking

21 MOUNTAIN: Proceed with caution, roadblocks at work, stubborn coworker, setbacks cause suspicion, limited work, obstacle is caused by manipulation, pyramid scheme, remote work, hardened employee, challenging job

22 PATH: Decisions at work, several jobs, duplicity, unusual coworker, choice of job, possible employment, planning out a job, roadwork, alternative work, on the route to work, planning your career, unfamiliar job, options presented at work

23 MICE: Downsizing at work, stressful job, decreased work hours, employee theft, workplace robbery, thick as thieves, gnawing suspicion, modern-day Bonnie and Clyde, being eaten away by guilt, corruption at work, less work, wearing down for easy manipulation (gaslighting)

24 HEART: Romantic scam, well-loved job, passionate career, love eludes you, relationship guilt, love is tricky, caution, charity work, a philanthropist

25 RING: Contract work, the deal is tricky, agreement is misleading, contract job, committed to your job, workaholic (continuously working), marriage scam, offer of employment

26 BOOK: Secrets revealed at work, information is manipulated, researching a job, education scam, a publisher, a teacher, an academic, a librarian, a bookkeeper, an author

27 LETTER: Letter of employment, résumé, job offer, postal worker, writer, results are manipulated, texting behind your back, messaging on the sly, scheduled work, propaganda, writing gig

28 MAN: Cunning man, sly man, red-haired man, con man, sneaky man, manipulative man, shallow man, guilty man, male coworker, male employee, working man

29 WOMAN: Shrewd woman, sneaky female, red-haired woman, con artist, foxy lady, scheming woman, manipulative woman, guilty woman, female co-worker, female employee, fake woman, superficial lady, working woman

30 LILY: Mature employee, experienced worker, elder fraud, skilled worker, winter job, private job, established career, retiring from work, private job, "silver fox"

31 SUN: Successful career, getting the job, positive employee, time-share scam, thriving at work, opportunist, good worker, exposing fraud, good job, vacation scam, day shift, an electrician, survival, getting it done!

32 MOON: Moonlighting, creative work, feeling guilty, aware of the scam, a psychiatrist, a psychic, emotional manipulation, the night shift, emotional co-worker

33 KEY: Karma at work, important work, freelance worker, prestigious title, good strategy, key employee, a politician, finding a way to survive, access to work, ritual work

34 FISH: Financial fraud, phishing scam, business fraud, financial employee, business employee, investment scam, an accountant, money fraud, wages from work, pricing a job

35 ANCHOR: Stable job, securing employment, long-term employment, waterworks, job security, routine job, a mariner, establishing the groundwork, steady job, stuck at work, solid career, persisting guilt

36 CROSS: Burdened by work, agonizing guilt, regretting your job, difficult coworker, charity work, victim of fraud, enslaved to your job, religious cult, suffering at work, burnout from working, disappointing job, exhausting job, shame and guilt, responsibility at work

> *Never trust a fox. Looks like a dog, behaves like a cat.*
> —*Erin Hunter*

15 Bear

You know when I'm coming, the ground will shake with might
A mama protecting her cubs, I will never run from a fight
Large and fearless I growl, powerfully overbearing I can be
Following the song of my heart, as my Spirit roams free

KEYWORDS:

Large, Powerful, Mother, Grandmother, Dominant, Well built, Mighty, Food, Obese, Big, Aggressive, Strength, Weight, Boss/manager, Overbearing, Formidable, Diet, Force, Leader

MEANING:

The Bear brings a considerable amount of force and power into any situation. Like a big exclamation mark that makes you turn your head and take notice. Associated with aggression and strength, the Bear card is a leader and represents the head of the clan, and the matriarch of the family.

Lenormand Bear Combinations

1 RIDER: Delivering food, the news is powerful, big news, visit from the boss, announcement from management, arrival of strength, fast food, visit from Mom

2 CLOVER: Luck is strong, winning big, temporary manager, casual dieter, happy-go-lucky boss, small gain (weight), a short burst of power

3 SHIP: Traveling boss, foreign power, seafood, imported food, foreign boss, distant mother, slacking off from a diet, a tour leader, a captain

4 HOUSE: Mansion, refrigerator, house mother, family matriarch, house is built strong, a property manager, a landlord, family strength, pantry, kitchen

5 TREE: Diet, obesity, growing stronger, healthful weight, healthy and strong, medical authority, spiritual strength, mitochondrial DNA (mtDNA), ancestral matriarch, a spiritual leader, a life coach

6 CLOUDS: Hidden eating disorder, troubling weight, troubled boss, sadness is overbearing, hiding food, misunderstanding with the mother-in-law, depression is overbearing, misunderstanding with the boss, confused management, mindful eating

7 SNAKE: Jealous manager, treacherous mother-in-law, desire is forced, toxic boss, desiring power, transforming your body through dieting, craving food, lying boss

8 COFFIN: Loss of power, ending a diet, morbid obesity, buried food issues, bad mother, no food, expired food, loss of a matriarch, a negative mother-in-law, a bad boss, final weigh-in, empty fridge or pantry, negative manager

9 BOUQUET: Nice restaurant, pleasant manager, invite to join a weight-loss program, a diet, liposuction, grateful boss, colorful matriarch, appreciation for food, Thanksgiving, grateful for the meal, charming boss, makeover, flexing your muscles

10 SCYTHE: Gathering power, sudden weight gain, gathering forces, cutting calories, gastric bypass (surgery), cutting the power, dangerous boss, collecting food

11 WHIP: Using sexual force, yo-yo dieting, abusive manager, critical boss, sexual aggression, sexually overbearing, a dominatrix, a personal trainer, a bodybuilder, criticizing your weight

12 BIRDS: Stressed about weight, speaking powerfully, phone call from the boss, talking about diets, gossiping about management, nervous mother, gossip is powerful, talking to the boss

13 CHILD: Inexperienced manager, a child's mother or grandmother, small portions of food, newfound power, young mother, new diet, small menu, immature manager, tiny restaurant, new food, new boss, new menu, new mom

14 FOX: Sneaky boss, scheming management, manipulative boss, the workforce, unreliable strength, suspicious mother-in-law, outsmarting the boss, work is overbearing, unreliable management, established restaurant

16 STARS: Inspirational boss, hopeful leader, a mentor, celebrity chef, inspirational matriarch, social-media influencer, Dream Big!

17 STORK: Change in management, seasonal menu, changing your diet, returning boss, slim build, seasonal fruits and vegetables, shift in power

18 DOG: Trusting your boss, protective mother, an advisor, a counselor, reliable boss, a nutritionist, loyal manager, supportive management, watching what you eat

19 TOWER: The highest authority, lonely boss, official force, a judge, prime minister, Supreme Court, egotistical boss, a dean, government authority, political leader, self-serving management, controlling boss, a stubborn boss

20 GARDEN: Outdoor dining, group leader, outdoor catered event, group effort, garden bounty, publicly at large, open air market, farmers' market, meeting with the boss, fad diet

21 MOUNTAIN: Tough management, stalled weight loss, stone-faced boss, distant boss, harsh manager, blocked power, intermittent fasting, harsh leader, restricted diet

22 PATHS: Unusual diet, choosing a diet, choices are overbearing, decision brings strength, unconventional boss, planning a meal

23 MICE: Slimming down, decrease in power, corrupt management, weakening, worried boss, stealing food, losing weight, declining strength, worried mother, sabotaging a diet, the "Big Cheese"

24 HEART: Compassionate leader, love is strong, spoiled food, relationship is strong, foodie (loves food), loving mother or grandmother, generous boss, kind manager

25 RING: The bond is strong, contract is powerful, well-rounded boss, commitment is strong, round physique, proposition from the boss

26 BOOK: Mysterious force, knowledgeable boss, studying nutrition, a tutor, mysterious power, researching diets, educated boss, a headmaster, smart leader, closet eater

27 LETTER: Email from the boss, communication is forced, a menu, communicating with your manager, letter from Grandma, correspondence from your boss, message from Mom, email from management

28 MAN: Powerful man, dominant man, forceful man, obese man, bearded man, boss man, overbearing man, muscular man, large man, big man, overweight man, hairy man, strong man

29 WOMAN: Mother, a grandmother, mother figure, formidable woman, dominant lady, pushy lady, curvy girl, boss lady, overbearing woman, large woman, overweight woman, strong woman, obese woman

30 LILY: A grandmother, peaceful leader, well-aged wine, old food, a polar bear, retired boss, calm manager, experienced leader, mature manager, old boss

31 SUN: Great boss, abundance of power, successful diet, solar power, day manager, good food, positive boss, confident leader, conscious eating, good mother

32 MOON: Emotional strength, manifesting power, emotional eater, creative boss, intuitive mother, high priestess, night manager, influential boss, mystical power

33 KEY: Karmic forces, significant force, distinguished leader, important boss, key matriarch, open manager, access to power

34 FISH: Business tycoon, financial manager, sugar mama, flow of power, spending power, buying power, spending money on diets, financial strength

35 ANCHOR: Heavy weight, maintaining your weight, steady force, staying power, holding on to power, routine diet, grounding force

36 CROSS: The burden is overbearing, obligated in a big way, a religious leader, disappointing management, spirit animal (the Bear), testing your strength, painful aggression, difficult boss, burned-out boss, very overbearing, the cross you bear

Teddy bears never forget, but we do!
—Anthony T. Hincks

16 Stars

Looking for my North Star, a wish held in my heart
Every fateful journey begins, the moment you start
Look to the Stars for guidance, inspired by your dreams
Steadily moving forward, until the universe intervenes

KEYWORDS

Wishes, Hope, Dreams, Potential, Guidance, Inspiration, Philosophy, Exposure, Align, Bright, Vision, Science, Fame, Highest, Blessings, World Wide Web, Technology, Electricity, Clarity, Recognition, Aspirations, Universe, Unlimited, Harmony, Uplifting, Positive, High, Goals, Visible, Future, Eternal, North

MEANING

When the Stars come shining into your life, blessings abound. This is a very favorable card to see in a reading, having a very fortunate effect on any situation and positively influencing all the surrounding cards.

Lenormand Stars Combinations

1 RIDER: News feed, news is uplifting, announcement is optimistic, the encounter has potential, going in your favor, famous visitor, mobile internet

2 CLOVER: Very optimistic, situation is very hopeful, lucky star, sudden insight, gambling site, luck is at a high, Lady Luck shines on you, cheerful optimism, opportunity has potential, spontaneous vision, lucky dream

3 SHIP: Charting a course, journey to fame, exploring your dreams, camping, travel site, journey north, following your North Star, your "guiding light"

4 HOUSE: The house has potential, home up north, social-media page, real estate site, home's internet, family harmony, family has hope, real estate dreams, family blessings, real estate goals

5 TREE: Spiritual guidance, recovery, prognosis is positive, ancestor's guidance, body positive, health improves, diagnosis is optimistic, health is radiant, healthful goals, soul-searching, growing inspiration

6 CLOUDS: Clouded hope, confusing goals, hidden dreams, cloud technology, doubting potential, obscured vision, feeling exposed, vague goals, addiction is exposed, clouded visibility, overcast sky

7 SNAKE: Cheating exposed, lie uncovered, desiring inspiration, enemy becomes apparent, female celebrity, infamous, pipe dreams, the Other Woman is exposed, problematic goals

8 COFFIN: No hope, letting go of a dream, dying wish, bad Wi-Fi, empty hope, death wish, blackout (electrical), final wish, no future, burying your potential, no electricity, ending your dreams, uninspired, neutral

9 BOUQUET: Blossoming hope, beautiful dreamer, beautiful blessing, modeling, eastern star, sweet dreams, gratitude, celebrity, stars, thank your lucky stars

10 SCYTHE: Cutting off hope, suddenly clear, detached from one's potential, cutting off the electricity, disconnecting Wi-Fi, broken dreams, dangerously exposed, accident prone, dividing your goals, defamed, damaged reputation

11 WHIP: Workout goals, abuse is exposed, porn site, pattern of the stars, sexual high, sexually exposed, critical of goals, intermittent electricity, disrupting harmony, a porn star, conflicting dreams, indecent exposure

12 BIRDS: Conversation is hopeful, couple goals, conversation is insightful, anxious about the future, whispering words of inspiration, tweets, music, discussion is invigorating, talking about goals

13 CHILD: Fresh inspiration, new hope, born under a lucky star, born to shine, small goals, new vision, child star, new goal, little bit of fame, childhood dream

14 FOX: False hope, employment potential, career goals, employment site, employee recognition, tricky aspiration, elusive dream, misleading guidance, scam exposed, manipulating science

15 BEAR: Big dreams, powerful guidance, powerful awakening, weight-loss inspiration, big plans, maternal guidance, strongly motivated

17 STORK: Improving, birth chart, changing your goals, evolving dream, moving toward your goals, birth of a star

18 DOG: Protecting your dreams, reliable guidance, following your dreams, supporting your vision, help in achieving your goals, followers (social media), friendly motivation

19 TOWER: Reach for the stars, self-serving goals, established goals, uplifting, great heights, high ambition, head of guidance, elevation, a satellite, a skyscraper, official fame, ambitious goals, past dreams, the time is NOW!

20 GARDEN: Public exposure, public figure, public event, group harmony, team vision, team goals, networking, paparazzi, stargazing, social network, gathering inspiration

21 MOUNTAIN: Blocked potential, challenging goals, restricted internet, blocking your view, obstacles to your goal, very far away, blocked dreams, distant star, rockstar, obstructing your vision, limited guidance, putting off your dreams

22 PATHS: Choice is positive, decision has potential, path is clear, path to enlightenment, choice is clear, possibility is hopeful, unusual goal, strange dream, choosing goals

23 MICE: Dwindling hope, stolen dreams, pessimistic, losing hope, flawed diamond, stealing Wi-Fi, decreased potential, disrupted harmony, destructive dreams, lessening fame, ruined reputation, corrupt guidance, lessening influence

24 HEART: Blessed love, dating site, relationship goals, relationship improves, romantic potential, love chart (astrology), relationship potential

25 RING: Offer is positive, promise will be fulfilled, deal is hopeful, the planets, deal is positive, connecting electricity, dedicated to your goals, committed to your vision

26 BOOK: Secrets are exposed, educational goals, the Akashic records, studying sciences/philosophy, unknown potential, secret dreams, secret hopes, studying astrology

27 LETTER: It's written in the stars, text messages, email, writing down your goals, letter of recommendation, letter of reference, letter of acceptance, writing affirmations, results are positive, written schedule

28 MAN: Famous man, male influencer, inspiring man, hopeful man, positive man, goal-oriented man, dreamer, visionary, optimistic man, good-natured man, man of your dreams, philosophical man

29 WOMAN: Famous woman, female influencer, inspiring female, hopeful woman, positive lady, goal-oriented woman, dreamer, visionary, optimistic woman, good-natured lady, dream girl, enlightened woman

30 LILY: Peaceful night, retirement goals, old as the stars, discretion needed, fatherly advice, retirement goals, old dream, retirement dream

31 SUN: Great potential, very positive, bright future, a Leo, happiness, dawn, equal, warm wishes, fireworks, shooting stars, shinning star, restoring your dreams, winner, renewed inspiration, truth is clear, achieving your goals, thriving future, hotspot (Wi-Fi)

32 MOON: Astrology, recognition, manifesting your dreams, spells or intentions, imagine, psychic vision, celebrity, influenced, precognitive dream, night vision, psychic vision, reflecting on your goals, the night sky, dreams

33 KEY: Answer is clear, achieving your goals, freedom to dream, important dream, destined for fame, open Wi-Fi, important vision, opened to receiving blessings, noble aspirations, open to guidance, revealing your goals, unlocking your potential

34 FISH: Shopping spree, earning potential, business goals, current of electricity, money flows unlimited, abundance, financial goals, flowing inspiration, financial guidance, earning money online

35 ANCHOR: Long-term goals, solid vision, holding on to your goals, lasting fame, stable electricity, grounding, steady guidance, eternal, persisting dream, a constant wish, sticking to your philosophy, stable prospect

36 CROSS: Testing your faith, hopelessness, suffering from too much exposure, the obligation is clear, Spirit in the sky, supernova, burdened beyond belief, taxed by celebrity, religious blessing, enslaved by religion, worshiping the stars

We are all star stuff. —Carl Sagan

17 Stork

A spark of a brand-new life, cresting into existence
Movement and change, cycles met with persistence
Nurturing love gingerly, swaddled into a bundle of joy
Carrying a precious little girl, or a bouncing baby boy

KEYWORDS

Change, Migration, Birth, Seasonal, Transition, Progress, Trend, Shift, Evolve, Relocation, Graceful, Cycles, Moving, Spring, Rearrange, Quiet, Returns, Altered, Transfer

MEANING

When the Stork comes swooping into your life, it brings a noted change. The current situation is going to be altered; take a look at the surrounding cards to deduce if it will be a change for the good, or a change for the worse. The Stork card also represents births, new cycles, and movement.

Lenormand Stork Combinations

1 RIDER: News brings upheaval, messenger of birth, news of progress, movement, a suitor returns, announcing a move, comings and goings, news of a transfer

2 CLOVER: Small opportunity for change, springtime, luck returns, temporary move, opportunity to move, easy transition, quick progress, short cycle, lucky streak

3 SHIP: Winds of change, directional shift, transition, major movement, an expat, travel plans change, long-distance move, traveling to new location, traveling to the same destination year after year

4 HOUSE: Family dynamic changes, relocation, renovations, family member returns, real estate market changes, property transfer, comfortable transition

5 TREE: Thriving, healthy birth, fertility, menstrual cycle, healthful progress, human gene transfer, DNA transfer, health changes, life changes, spiritual shift, spiritually evolved

6 CLOUDS: Uncertain changes, rainy season, fearing change, confusing progress, moody, restlessness, doubtful move, confusing cycle, hidden transfer, wet spring, troubling relocation

7 SNAKE: Craving change, lying about progress, complicated move, difficult transition, toxic move, transformative change, complex move, challenging transformation

8 COFFIN: The last move, no change, end of season, miscarriage, negative move, bad pregnancy, completing a cycle, end of progress, final transition, ending a pregnancy, empty nest

9 BOUQUET: Appearance is altered, gift exchange, pleasant change, makeover, beautiful transition, surprising move, invitation to a baby shower, fashion trend, appearances change

10 SCYTHE: Quick transition, dangerous cycle, unexpected move, separated at birth, dangerous move, abortion, sudden change, irrevocable change, C-section, breaking the cycle

11 WHIP: Repetitive cycles, continual changes, aggressive transition, habitual mover, questionable move, a sex change, recurring sporting events (the Olympics, World Cup, etc.), conflict progresses

12 BIRDS: Talks about moving, discussing changes, hectic move, nervous about change, migrations, making exciting progress, negotiating a transfer, nervous about moving, excited for spring

13 CHILD: Pregnancy, new transition, beginning a new cycle, premature birth, new location, new trend, slight change, growing trend

14 FOX: Seasonal work, job transfer, surviving change, faking a pregnancy, sneaky movements, tricky move, suspicion returns, work in progress, caution with any change!

15 BEAR: Powerful shift, huge transition, aggressive move, powerful changes, big change, forceful transition, powerful trends, making a big move

16 STARS: Hoping for change, positive changes, harmonious transition, "a star is born," positive move, clear action is taken, universal shift

18 DOG: Friendship evolves, faithful return, trusting change, a doula, fur baby, trust the process, familiar cycle, a friend moves

19 TOWER: Ambitious change, official move, looking ahead, past progress, someone from the past returns, ordered to move, government changes, very tall, rules change, independent move

20 GARDEN: Public change, social change, public movement, societal shifts, meeting progress, culture change, group progress, a crowd, popular trend, social life shifts

21 MOUNTAIN: Resisting change, blocked progress, overdue pregnancy, delayed progress, limited progress, putting off a move, avoiding change, hard transition, challenging move

22 PATHS: Choosing to change, the road traveled, unusual move, option to relocate, strange trend, possible pregnancy, planning the next move, planned pregnancy, alternate path

23 MICE: Diminished progress, costly move, worried about pregnancy, stressful change, devolved, ruined progress

24 HEART: Love returns, affection evolves, relationship progress, flirting with change, monogamy, faithfulness

25 RING: Continual changes, continual cycle, promising change, predictable move, going in circles, agreement changes, deal progresses, recurring trends, proposing change, committed to change, circulating through cycles

26 BOOK: Secretive movements, secret pregnancy, school semester, historical movement, wise move, informative move, unknown progress, editing, journaling, book exchange, history repeats itself

27 LETTER: Schedule, messages exchanged, file transfer, evident change, schedule changes, message causes change, results change, printing cycle

28 MAN: A man returns, tall man, transitioning male, evolved man, sophisticated man, monogamous man, quiet man, caring man, graceful man, progressive man, restless man

29 WOMAN: A woman returns, tall woman, transitioning female, evolved woman, sophisticated lady, monogamous woman, quiet lady, caring woman, graceful lady, progressive woman, classy lady, restless woman

30 LILY: Wintertime migration, peaceful transition, evolved, winter season, aging process, snowbirds, discreet move, measurable progress

31 SUN: Successful change, courageous move, real change, rebirth, warmth returning, good move, winning move, energetic shift, summertime, the light returns, winning cycle, consciously evolving

32 MOON: Moon phases (cycles), feelings change, psychic shift, creative progress, emotional shift, recognizable changes, intentions evolve, monthly cycle

33 KEY: Significant changes, open to change, major transition, important move, key changes, karmic cycle, karma returns (what goes around comes around)

34 FISH: Circulating through cycles, money laundering, business evolves, business relocation, fluctuating change, finances change, money transfer, flowing through cycles

35 ANCHOR: Stuck in transition, tides of change, the anchor shifts, staying put, stable changes, steady progress, heavy move, a serious change

36 CROSS: Difficult change, obligated to change, disappointing move, necessary move, regretting a move, tax returns, tired of moving, painful transition, having to go through it, religion evolves

Consciousness is only possible through change;
change is only possible through movement.
—Aldous Huxley

18 Dog

Loyal faithful companion, man's greatest friend
Unconditional love given, until the very end
Valiant watchful guardian, will forfeit his life for you
The heart of a dog is patient, helpful, devoted, and true

KEYWORDS

Friend, Loyal, Follower, Reliable, Helper, Companion, Support, Investigation, Guide, Submissive, Faithful, Dependable, Protection, Watchful, Guard, Trustworthy, Familiar, a Pet, Unconditional, Obedient, Service

MEANING

When the Dog bounds into your life it usually represents someone who is familiar to you, such as friends or even acquaintances. The Dog represents someone who will enter your life and be of service and very helpful to you.

Lenormand Dog Combinations

1 RIDER: Visit from a friend, arrival of help, news about a friend, a horse, arrival of a pet, speedy support, active dog, declaration of support

2 CLOVER: Gambling friend, short-term assistance, brief friendship, lucky instinct, casual friendship, funny friend, fleeting support, easy to trust, light-hearted friendship, casual observation, spontaneous friendship, informal investigation, happy-go-lucky friend

3 SHIP: Travel buddy, foreign friend, tour guide, long-distance friendship, international investigation, saying goodbye to a friend, navigating a friendship, foreign aid, travel protection

4 HOUSE: Family pet, family protection, home inspection, family loyalty, family friend, doghouse, real estate search, house alarm, house-sitting, domestic help

5 TREE: Medical examination, marking your territory, extreme patience, spiritual guidance, growing friendship, arborist, healthcare practitioner, growing trust, long-standing support, healthful friendship, body odor, spiritual support, therapy, spiritual coach

6 CLOUDS: Confusing friendship, falling out with a friend, mental health examination, imaginary friend, hidden friendship, troubled friend, fair-weather friend, lack of details sparks an investigation, unclear support, misunderstanding between friends

7 SNAKE: Betrayed by a friend, jealous friend, lying friend, desiring your friend, selfish friend, rivalry, twisted friend, attracted to your friend, toxic friend, dishonest friend, bitch

8 COFFIN: Ending a friendship, grief counselor, ending an investigation, bad friend, final outcome of an investigation, mourning a friend, ill friend, sick like a dog, negative friend, no friends, not reliable, no support, nonexistent friendship, coroner, an autopsy, ending support, not to be trusted!

9 BOUQUET: Beautiful friendship, pleasant friendship, inviting friends, grateful for friends, surprising a friend, a botanist, gorgeous friend, show dog, appreciating your friendship, designer pet, snapdragon

10 SCYTHE: Cutting off a friend, dangerous friendship, homicide investigation, cutting off support, dangerous investigation, broken friend, unexpected friendship, collecting friends, broken dog

11 WHIP: Abusive friend, arguing with a friend, violating trust, critical friend, sexual assault investigation, questionable friend, subordinate, controlling friend, sex with a friend, angry friend

12 BIRDS: "Barking dogs" (gossiping friends), naturally curious, nosy, talking about a friend, chatting with a friend, couple friends, negotiating support

13 CHILD: New puppy, small dog, childhood friend, child protection services investigation, new friend, very playful, beginning a new friendship, little help, inexperienced friend, naive friend

14. FOX: Manipulative friend, disloyalty, superficial friendship, work friend, a coworker is watching you, fake friend, untrustworthy friend, working on your friendship, employee support, working dog, sneaky friend, primal instincts

15 BEAR: Powerful protection, large following, big dog, strong friendship, big investigation, weight-loss buddy, overbearing friend, powerful support, weight-loss coach, big help

16 STARS: A socialite, stargazing, famous friend, inspirational friend, multiple friends, online friends, divine protection, guide dog, universal guidance, online support, positive friend, your best friend

17 STORK: Changing loyalties, altering support, a changing friendship, cycling through friends, a birth coach, a pregnant friend, an evolving friendship, a returning friend

19 TOWER: Official follower, formal friendship, high school friend, top dog, government support, legal investigation, watchdog, lonely friend, past friendship, arrogant friend, controlling friend, official support

20 GARDEN: Group of friends, your network, public investigation, contact tracing, social-media followers, public support, meeting friends, gathering support, a pack, public protection, a club, neighborhood watch

21 MOUNTAIN: Challenging friendship, border protection, difficult investigation, a Saint Bernard, difficult friendship, delayed support, cut off from friends, getting the cold shoulder from a friend, a boarder collie, stubborn friend

22 PATHS: Parting ways with a friend, a stalker, multiple investigations, unusual friendship, multiple friends, possible friendship, planning assistance, follow your nose!

23 MICE: Dissipating loyalty, losing followers, dirty dog, fading friendship, dirty cop, stressful friendship, losing friends, user, ruining a friendship, less support, corrupt friend, diminished trust

24 HEART: Loyal friend, faithful companion, beloved pet, relationship therapy, heart dog, loving friendship, falling in love with your friend, affectionate friendship, generous friend, compassionate aid, in love with your best friend, romantic friendship

25 RING: Dedication, devotion, loyalty, dedicated support, circle of friends, commitment, bound by loyalty, ownership (rings, a dog collar), the circle of trust, ring of protection, marriage therapy, promise of help

26 BOOK: Learning to trust, secret friendship, research, study buddy, book editor, school friends, book club, training a dog, knowledgeable friend, secret investigation, a bookkeeper, tutoring, remembering a friend

27 LETTER: Text or email from a friend, letter of support, message offering help, sending help, scheduled therapy, card of support, sending help, message of support, messaging a friend

28 MAN: Faithful man, submissive man, friendly man, helpful man, loyal man, dependable man, trustworthy man, familiar man, male friend, supportive man, policeman

29 WOMAN: Faithful woman, known female, submissive female, friendly woman, helpful lady, loyal woman, dependable woman, trustworthy woman, familiar woman, female friend, supportive woman, policewoman

30 LILY: Elderly friend, discreet friendship, old friend, old dog, private investigator, cold case, mature friend, sage advice, lifelong friend, lifetime support, discreet investigation, established support

31 SUN: Good friend, happy friendship, successful friend, good dog, good friendship, successful investigation, confidante, welcomed help, true friend, renewed support, daily support, successful therapy, vacationing with a friend, sun protection

32 MOON: Intuitive friend, emotional friend, codependence, a familiar, psychic investigator, emotional support, creative friend, emotional support dog, influenced by a friend

33 KEY: A soulmate, important friendship, significant friend, open to help, karmic friendship, open investigation, key friend, access to aid, destined friendship, open to protection, answers revealed

34 FISH: Financial support, financial investigation, wealthy friend, deep friendship, a water dog, financial audit, business support, financial advisor, resourceful friend, financial protection, drinking buddy, insurance, business associate, business coach

35 ANCHOR: Reliable support, routine investigation, stable friendship, routine therapy, constant support, dependable friend, long-lasting friendship

36 CROSS: Burdened by a friend, priest, spirit hunter, critical help, disappointing friendship, devotional service, religious friend, a critical investigation, exhausting friendship, spirit guide, difficult friend, religious support, regretting a friendship, devout follower

The face of a golden retriever feels like home.
—David Rosenfelt

19 Tower

Isolated and proud stands the ancient Tower
A rigid sight to behold, full of arrogance and power
Traditions of old, from lofty heights it is ruling
The authority of the realm, aloof and self-serving

KEYWORDS

Loneliness, Official, Withdrawn, Rigid, Ego, Arrogance, Ambition, Formal, the Past, Authority, Solitude, Defending, Institution, Aloof, Governing bodies, Tall structures, Building, Rules, an Old Man, Established, Traditional, Isolated, Up, Control, Enforced, Judgment, Self-absorbed, Defending

MEANING

The Tower is a rigid, proud structure, a building that is built to stand the test of time. The Tower can denote an actual establishment representing something official or formal. The Tower permeates with an air of aloofness and self-importance.

Lenormand Tower Combinations

1 RIDER: News is official, swift ruling, on a high horse, movements are aloof, quick ruling, young man is arrogant, notifying the authorities, suitor from the past, post office, news from the past

2 CLOVER: Gaming official, opportunity arises from the past, second chance, casino, gaming authority, funny tradition, the house rules (casino)

3 SHIP: Traveling alone, exploring solitude, searching for solace, distance causes loneliness, lighthouse, travel authority, consulate, travel agency, foreign official, far from home and lonely

4 HOUSE: Multilevel dwelling, real estate office, family isolation, family traditions, real estate building, domestic structure

5 TREE: Health organization, medical building, hospital, growing ambition, healthy ego, extended isolation, spine or back, doctor's office, health officials, healing the past, spiritual center

6 CLOUDS: Narcissist, doubting authority, anarchy, hiding loneliness, hiding the past, mind control, lawlessness, confused by the rules, troubled past, clouded judgment, weather beacon (tower)

7 SNAKE: Great ambition, desiring approval, enemy of the state, lying about the past, toxic organization, bending the rules, dishonest organization, egotistical, self-absorbed, lying official

8 COFFIN: Grieving alone, end of ambition, ending loneliness, ending traditions, morgue, bad government, confinement, death registry, coroner, bad organization, no rules, shutting down an organization, death of an old man, letting go of the past

9 BOUQUET: Vanity, very conceited, show-off, eastern tower, showing signs of loneliness, salon, gift registry, cosmetic surgeon's office, art gallery, shopping center, medi-spa

10 SCYTHE: Sudden withdrawal, risky ambition, immediate justice, circumcision, vasectomy, dropping out of school, breaking the rules, judgment, severing the past, dangerous organization

11 WHIP: Gym, sports center, aggressive ambition, inquisition, abusing authority, sexual past, abuse of power, egomaniac, penis, punishment is stiff, exercise regiment, enforcing the rules, questionable organization, conflict escalates, sexually heightened

12 BIRDS: Loud mouth, airport, the Twin Towers, gossiping about the past, oral traditions, legal discussions or negotiations, flying high, restless in isolation, control tower, recording studio, radio station, talking about yourself

13 CHILD: Child services, immature ambition, childhood, adoption agency, small penis, playing by the rules, new rules, starting a new tradition, a little bit arrogant, fragile ego, underestimating authority

14 FOX: Working for the government, clever organization, sneaky official, eluding isolation, escaping a prison, untrustworthy government, fraudulent organization, manipulating the rules, guilty!

15 BEAR: Natural leader, restaurant, massively overbearing, judge, large penis, food building or factory, powerful government official, big ego, overbearing

16 STARS: Skyscraper, cellular tower, satellite, movie or TV studio, antenna, high up, high ambitions, inspirational organization, exposing the past

17 STORK: Tall building, changing of the guard, changing the past, move causes loneliness, changing the rules, changing traditions, birth registry

18 DOG: Following the rules, familiar loneliness, closely guarding the past, follow your ambition, friendly old man, watchtower, following traditions, a warden, police headquarters, protective custody, friendly official

20 GARDEN: Public duty, municipal building, conference, public authority, public company, a union, social isolation, public building, crowd control, public registry, public archive, social practices, social justice

21 MOUNTAIN: Challenging authority, very withdrawn, difficult past, border control, stubborn old man, obstruction of the law, red tape, extreme isolation, withdrawn, cut off, unyielding, challenging the rules, mountain climbing, extreme stubbornness, permanent structure, hard rules, delayed sentencing

22 PATHS: Choosing isolation, decision is firm, elections, deciding on the rules, unusual organization, unfamiliar rules, choosing traditions

23 MICE: Corrupt authority, selfish, dwindling authority, crumbling tower, fading traditions, obsessed with politics, the piper, corrupt government, decreased pride, prison, dirty building, diminished ego

24 HEART: Loving solitude, longing, affection is withdrawn, loving tradition, lonely, loving isolation, relationship rules, generous government, kind official, lover from the past

25 RING: Bound by bureaucracy, solemn oath, bound by pride, marriage registry, bound by traditions, bound by the rules, the deal is sealed, marriage ceremony, wedding official

26 BOOK: Library, Akashic records, publishing house, remembering the past, historical traditions, secret past, educational authority, college/university, historical archives, secretive government, academic ambition, academia, unknown past, secret organization

27 LETTER: Written policy, message is aloof, written rules & regulations, transcription, written paper archives, written statement, report card, letter from the government

28 MAN: Ambitious man, traditional man, man from the past, egotistical man, arrogant man, lonely man, proud man, imposing man, formal man, established man, controlling man

29 WOMAN: Ambitious woman, traditional woman, woman from the past, selfish woman, princess in the tower, haughty lady, lonely female, intimidating woman, established woman, controlling woman, self-absorbed lady

30 LILY: Peaceful solitude, old-fashioned, private company, ancient sites, old building, private organization, museum, your old self, the past, old traditions, seniors in isolation

31 SUN: Successful organization, winning a court case, solar tower, thriving establishment, being alone, willfulness, confidence, truth about the past

32 MOON: Influenced by the past, feeling isolated, recognizing authority, emotionally withdrawn, night court, coerced by an official, emotionally withdrawn, bribing an official, aware of the rules

33 KEY: Ruler, freedom, karmic past, chief authority, open-door policy, get-out-of-jail-free card, breakthrough, opening up, revealing the past, respected organization

34 FISH: Financial institution, shopping center, deep loneliness, money snob, fishing authorities, financial controller, financial past, business rules & regulations, alcoholic withdrawal

35 ANCHOR: Secure defense, unyielding, long-term confinement, long-lasting traditions, long-lasting isolation, serious loneliness, lockdown

36 CROSS: Taxes, doctrine, religiously devout, religious building/structure, obligatory quarantine, burden of authority, church registry, strain of isolation, suffering alone, witch trials (a witch hunt), spirit from the past

Things always seem fairer when we look back at them, and it is out of that inaccessible tower of the past that Longing leans and beckons.
—James Russell Lowell

20 Garden

A beautiful place of splendor, gathering for a social affair
Sharing a sweet word, a coy glance, with a meaningful stare
An afternoon outing, a prearranged meeting in the park
A place where everyone will rendezvous and mingle until dark

KEYWORDS
Gatherings, Community, Meetings, Public, Groups, Social things, Crowd, Society, a Garden, Culture, Forum, Public Spaces, Events, Teamwork, Online places, Recreation, Social life, Festivals, Venue, Outdoors, Everybody, Social networks, Clubs

MEANING
When the Garden leisurely strolls into your life, it is indicative of a public place where groups of people go to enjoy themselves, decompress, and socialize with others.

Lenormand Garden Combinations

1 RIDER: Arrival of a group, announcing an event, movement of a group, suitor is a player, coming out to the public, quick meeting, the Other Man plays the field

2 CLOVER: Playing the field, lush green spaces, casual meeting, small opportunity to network, chance meeting, informal gathering, amusement park, fair or exhibition grounds, spontaneous get-together, lottery pool, lucky team, cheerful gathering, comedy club

3 SHIP: Traveling with a group, traveling somewhere lush and green, foreign culture, international group, traveling to an event, leaving a group

4 HOUSE: Neighborhood, real estate team, indoor/outdoor event, family gathering, home garden or yard, home and garden club, a domestic group, family clan

5 TREE: Lush garden, health conference, healing garden, growing network, health and wellness expo, haplogroups, growing garden, spiritual group, nudist park, health club

6 CLOUDS: Unorganized event, rain at an outdoor event, troublemakers, confusing everybody, confusing social life, vague meeting, troubled event, doubting the team, agoraphobia, hidden social life, hidden forum, disorderly crowd

7. SNAKE: Problematic event, snake in the grass, backstabbing group, transforming a green space, deceiving the public, mesmerizing a crowd, problems with neighbors, toxic group, complicated meeting

8 COFFIN: Canceled event, bad meeting, final gathering, leaving a group, nonexistent teamwork, preserving a culture, funeral, canceled meeting, cemetery, final resting place, negative group, stopping social gatherings

9 BOUQUET: Flower or herb garden, beautiful venue, surprise meeting, design team, art festival, get-together, invitation to a gathering, special meeting, blooming garden, invited to a group, horticulture club

10 SCYTHE: Reaping what you sow, impromptu gathering, division between people, cutting the grass, autumn festival, dangerous gathering, risky rendezvous, unsafe event, unexpected meeting, gathering a crowd

11 WHIP: A sports team, abusive group, workout group, questioning the public, arguing in public, exercise in the park, sex club, a sports club, aggressive group, exhibitionism, critical group, voyeurism, abusive crowd, violent gathering, serial dater

12 BIRDS: Speech, concert, hectic event, nervous crowd, lecture hall, concert in the park, gossip in the group, restless public, "birds of a feather flock together," music festival

13 CHILD: New event, small gathering, child's event, new social network, inexperienced team, scamming the public, playground, new social group, vulnerable group, small group

14 FOX: Suspicious gathering, unreliable team, swaying the public, sneaky team, work meeting, work event, work conference, workgroup, fake group, scheming network, manipulating the public

15 BEAR: Powerful social network, catered event, large assembly, food festival, large group, big crowd, power in numbers, big meeting, weight-loss group, powerful group, big meeting

16 STARS: Great event, online group, high society, online network, online meeting, online forum, inspirational meeting, "dream team," any online social platform, inspirational group, positive meeting

17 STORK: Change of venue, switch teams, seasonal crowd, regrouping, restless public, migrating group, seasonal event, spring festival, progressive group

18 DOG: Friendly gathering, support group, loyal network, friends with everyone, trust your team, dog pack, reliable team, following a group, protecting the public, friend on social media, dog park, kennel club

19 TOWER: Formal gathering, regulating the public, high-control group, constituents, parliament, established team, political party, formal garden, restricted social gathering, uptown, legal council, controlling the public

21 MOUNTAIN: Opposing team, blocking a group, challenging event, stubborn crowd, postponing an event, restricted area, blocking a crowd, remote meeting, distant group

22 PATHS: Multiple events, choosing a team, different group, unusual meeting, alternate venue, unfamiliar group, outdoors, pathways, multiple forums

23 MICE: Stressful meeting, worried public, neglected garden, worried about an event, wearing down the public, the collective, teamwork, everybody

24 HEART: Passionate team, charitable event, dating groups (online), generous crowd, liking a group on social media, dating sites, benevolent society, dating forum, dating, playing the field, likes on social media

25 RING: Wedding event, booking a venue, engagement party, contracted event, promising group, enclosed garden, dedicated team, exclusive club

26 BOOK: Study group, secret rendezvous, educating the public, secret group, informative meeting, secret network, publishing group, book club, secret forum, publicist, secret garden, secret social life, convocation, secret society, remember it's a secret!

27 LETTER: Newspaper, news about an event, flyer, blog, advertising, post on social media, writers' club, writers' group, results from a meeting, scheduled meeting

28 MAN: Player, male public figure, popular man, single man, playboy, cultured man, country boy, boy's club, uncommitted man, men in general, group of men, available man

29 WOMAN: Femme fatale, female public figure, socialite, party girl, popular woman, country girl, single lady, women in general, cultured woman, group of ladies, women's group, uncommitted female, available woman

30 LILY: Retirement community, private group, seniors' club, gentlemen's club, private event, old group, peaceful gathering, retirement event, mature team, experienced team, winter festival, private meeting

31 SUN: Successful meeting, popularity, the optimist club, effective team, confident team, thriving team, productive network, summer festival, warm reception, vetting a group, thriving garden, successful team, good meeting

32 MOON: Influencing the public, coven, magickal group, metaphysical fair, psychic forum, emotional meeting, moon garden, emotional group

33 KEY: Significant meeting, open to the public, key network, open forum, elite society, VIP group, important meeting, significant gathering, open meeting, prestigious club, open to everyone

34 FISH: Trade show, business conference, water park, company event, business meeting, business group, a bar, financial group, drinking in public, the Rotary Club, business conference

35 ANCHOR: Lengthy assembly, stable network, safety meeting, stuck in the middle, routine meeting, solid group, yacht club, dependable team, safety in numbers, downtown, stable team

36 CROSS: Religious group, necessary teamwork, religious forum, sacred space, regret joining the group, religious event, séance, straining the public, faith group, tough crowd, congregation, difficult meeting, disappointing group

Faeries are known to be tenders of plants and energizing inhabitants of gardens. —Elizabeth Eiler

21 Mountain

At an impasse you stand, for I am blocking your way
Timeless and distant I am, setbacks causing a delay
Presenting challenges and obstacles, with insurmountable odds
The stagnation of the Mountain, the sacred home of the Gods

KEYWORDS

Obstacles, Stillness, Challenges, Delays, Impasse, Distant, Permanence, Boundaries, Remote, Setbacks, Blocks, Limits, Obstruction, Stalled, Immovable, Hard, Harsh, Rough, Restricted, Interrupting, Stubborn

MEANING

When the Mountain makes an appearance, it will always represent an obstacle or a delay of some kind. The Mountains highlights a massive setback causing you to stop and take notice, purposely slowing you down

Lenormand Mountain Combinations

1 RIDER: Visitor is delayed, arrival is delayed, company overstays, delivery is delayed, news is challenging, access to the Other Man is blocked, suitor is being distant, the Other Man is being stubborn

2 CLOVER: Brief setback, luck is temporarily blocked, slight hesitation, brief delay, temporary obstruction, passing block, fleeting obstacle, an easy challenge, an easy obstacle, a brief pause

3 SHIP: Trip is postponed, foreign border, travel delays, movement is hampered, trip is put off, travel restrictions, at a great distance

4 HOUSE: Family boundaries, house in the mountains, family obstacles, real estate delay, house sale is stalled, house sitting on the market, real estate setback

5 TREE: Healthful boundaries, deeply rooted obstacle, healing crystals, health setback, medical procedure postponed, health remains unchanged, chakras are blocked

6 CLOUDS: Unknown block, hidden obstacle, obscure challenge, vagueness, confused by delays, eerie stillness, denial

7 SNAKE: Complicated obstacle, bowel obstruction, enemy is out of reach, pipes blocked, warning in the distance, transformation is put off

8 COFFIN: Unblocked, dead end, ending is delayed, ending of obstacles, a closed border, a headstone, ending distance, no interruption, no limits

9 BOUQUET: Improvements, easing of obstacles, cosmetic procedure is postponed, design challenge, invitation is delayed, beautiful moment of stillness, enjoying the distance

10 SCYTHE: Cut off at the pass, unexpected obstacle, vaccine setback, sudden delay, danger up ahead, cutoff, adversity, unexpected delay, sudden block, cutting out obstacles

11 WHIP: Pushing the limits, repeated delays, punished hard, questionable boundaries, sexually blocked, pattern of delays, practice is delayed, sexual boundaries, investigation reaches a dead end, arguments are harsh, punishment is steep

12 BIRDS: Talking remotely, conversation is interrupted, unsettling stillness, conversation is limited, negotiations are delayed, talking harshly, nervous at a border crossing

13 CHILD: Small obstacle, short delay, little hesitation, new obstacle, small challenge, new challenge, small hinderance, slight setback

14 FOX: Finding your way around obstacles, working remotely, workplace challenges, work issues, manipulating hard boundaries, a work-around, an employment setback

15 BEAR: Big obstacle, weight-loss plateau, big challenge, immense block, food issues, huge delay, weight-loss stall

16 STARS: Breathtaking view, higher perspective, seeing clearly, great distance away, eternal, timeless, reaching the top of the mountain, exposing limits, clearing obstacles

17 STORK: Relocating to the mountains, some movement, moving through obstacles, releasing a block, recurring delays, changing boundaries

18 DOG: Trust the delay, protective of boundaries, respecting limits, receiving help with challenges, keeping a friendly distance

19 TOWER: Legal challenges, confinement, Old Man Mountain, cockblocked, customs, authorized limits, very stubborn, a formal boundary, taking a rigid stance

20 GARDEN: Crowd limits, public obstruction, meeting is put off, social distancing, social boundary, social limits, a group event is delayed, a public event is postponed, a cultural boundary

22 PATHS: Path leading nowhere, roadblock, unusual restriction, hesitating on your path, decision is firm, unusual setback, possible challenge, multiple obstacles, alternative path up the mountain

23 MICE: Destroying limits, chipping away at obstacles, vanishing boundaries, crumbling mountain, lessening obstacles, worried about challenge, stressed about a delay, less restriction, removing barriers

24 HEART: Relationship is challenging, coronary blockage, relationship boundaries, love is forsaken, romantic setback, love is hard, heart of stone, relationship has its limits

25 RING: Agreement is permanent, marriage is challenging, contract is unbreakable, contract delay, engagement is put off, wedding is postponed, continuous obstacles, commitment is hard

26 BOOK: Secrets are well kept, school is put off, information is delayed, book is delayed, unknown hinderance, educational challenge, unknown boundaries, setting smart limits

27 LETTER: Written in stone, communication is blocked, correspondence interrupted, texts are limited, message is challenging, writer's block, newsletter is delayed, messages are blocked

28 MAN: Stubborn man, hard man, distant man, indifferent man, hostile man, rugged man, challenging man, mountain man, unavailable man, hard-to-reach man

29 WOMAN: Stubborn woman, disinterested woman, harsh woman, distant woman, nonchalant female, hostile woman, challenging female, unavailable woman, hard-to-reach woman

30 LILY: Retirement is postponed, cold shoulder, longevity, snowy mountain, avalanche, cold mountain, old man, old as the mountains, retirement challenges

31 SUN: Overcoming challenges, surmounting obstacles, renewing boundaries, reaching the summit, success, daily challenges, illuminating blocks

32 MOON: Creative block, being insensitive, feeling blocked, emotional block, intuitive block, reflecting on limitations, feeling the distance, emotional boundaries, aware of the obstacle

33 KEY: Significant delay, opening is revealed, substantial challenge, important boundary, freeing up blockages, opening up limitations, open border

34 FISH: Financial setback, business challenge, spending limits, funds are delayed, fishing is restricted, drinking is prohibited, business boundaries, resources are limited

35 ANCHOR: Permanence, stuck, long-lasting delay, heavy stillness, long-standing obstacle, heavily obstructed, hardly moving, stagnation, immovable, weighing heavily, solid rock

36 CROSS: Crucial delay, pilgrimage up a mountain, disappointing delay, transcendence, difficult obstacle, hardship, testing the limits, sacred stillness, exhausting challenges, difficult challenge

Over every mountain, there is a path, although it may not be seen from the valley. —Theodore Roethke

22 Paths

Two alternate Paths lie before you, separated by two
Possibilities presented, the decision is up to you
Left or right do you travel? A choice must come about
Be wise at the crossroads and choose the best route

KEYWORDS

Deciding, Road, Choice, Possibilities, Unusual, Pros & cons, Adventure, Alternative, Planning, Crossroads, Path, Multiple, Separation, Options, Unfamiliar, Different, the Way

MEANING

When the Paths come winding their way into your life, a choice of some kind will be presented before you. This decision must be must be made using your own volition.

Lenormand Paths Combinations

1 RIDER: The Other Man makes a choice, quick decision, arriving at a decision, moving along on your path, announcing your decision, visitors are on the way

2 CLOVER: Having fun on the road, lucky alternative, fortunate path, temporary choice, easy decision, spontaneous decision, lucky choice, informal decision, small opportunity on the way!

3 SHIP: Travel decision, a map, plotting your path, travel plans, traveling by road, journey, travel options, exploring your options, traveling in multiple directions, off the beaten path

4 HOUSE: Comfortable decision, renovation plans, family planning, real estate options, family decisions, house options, house plans

5 TREE: Medical decision, making healthful choices, life plan, nature walk, healthful options, blueprints, taking time to decide, recovery's a long road, patience in deciding

6 CLOUDS: Making a sad choice, undecided, disappointing choice, lost, very confused, troubled path, unclear path, remaining undecided, fluctuating path, confusing choice, indecisiveness, vague plan

7 SNAKE: Problematic path, flexible choice, long & winding road, fork in the road, beware there is an enemy on your path, transformative decision, twisted choice, wanting options, complicated decision, a labyrinth, the crooked path

8 COFFIN: Negative decision, no plan, no choice is made, bad plan, making final plans, end of the road, dead end, no options, no way out

9 BOUQUET: Positive decision, surprising choice, beautiful plan, design plan, eastern path, nice plan, presented with options, pleasing choice, decorating decisions

10 SCYTHE: Accident on the road, going down a dangerous road, carving out a path, separate path, dangerous plan, irrevocable decision, eliminating a choice, on a dangerous path, going separate ways, sudden decision, unexpected choice

11 WHIP: Disputing a decision, sexually adventurous, questionable decision, repetitive decisions, aggressive decision, bisexual, sexual decision, exercising your options, pros and cons, executing a plan, repeated many times

12 BIRDS: A pair, hectic decision, flight path, couple splits up, discussing plans, word on the street, voicing your decision, two options will be presented, talking options, either/or, couple of choices, uneasy decision

13 CHILD: Naive decision, short path, starting on your path, fresh possibilities, new options presented, immature decision, simple choice, small decision, new path, new plan

14 FOX: Career choices, tricky decision, wrong road, sneaky plan, work decision, instinctive choice, manipulating a decision, career path

15 BEAR: Big decision ahead, power to decide, food choices, powerful decision, big plans, diet plan, forced decision, strong possibility

16 STARS: Good choices, hopeful options, clear plan, guided decision, bright options, online options, clear choice, otherworldly, illuminating path, uplifting decision, taking the high road, guided path, dreaming of possibilities

17 STORK: Improvement, plan B, moving along the path, change of plans, a birth plan, changing your decision, progression, slim pickings, evolving options, altering your plans, moving forward, seasonal options

18 DOG: Friend's fallout, follow your path, guardian of the crossroads, trust your instincts, familiar choice, stand by your decision, dependable choice, on a reliable path, trust your decision

19 TOWER: Legal options, succession planning, official decision, elections, judgment, a ruling, executive decision, firm decision, authorized decision, legal verdict, formal choice, ambitious decision, making an official plan, past choice, government decision

20 GARDEN: Group decision, community planning, taking place outdoors, event planning, garden path, popular choice, public decision, mainstream options, gathering possibilities, green-space planning

21 MOUNTAIN: Mountain path, mountain stands in the way, bump on the road, hesitating on your path, blocking your way, at an impasse, the untrodden path, obstacle on your path, delayed decision, making a permanent decision, blocked path, hard choice, challenging plan

23 MICE: Vanishing options, the well-worn path, poor choice, collective decision, costly decision, opportunistic choice, ruined plans, destroying possibilities, corrupt decision, dirt path, lost your way

24 HEART: Uncommitted, relationship choices, going separate ways, making a passionate choice, heartfelt decision, relationship planning, pros and cons

25 RING: Marital decision, contract options, continual planning, exclusive option, endless possibilities, dedicated plan, proposed options, multiple contracts, inclusive choice, committing to a choice, agreed-upon decision

26 BOOK: Unknown options, informed decision, educational plan, unknown path, secret option, educational decision, making a secret decision, secret plans, researching pros and cons

27 LETTER: Written plan, making a list of pro and cons, marketing plan, advertising plan, list of options, advertising choices

28 MAN: Indecisive man, separated man, unfamiliar man, multiple men, unusual man, two-timing man, uncommitted man, alternative man, man on the road

29 WOMAN: Indecisive lady, separated woman, unfamiliar lady, multiple women, unusual woman, two-timing woman, uncommitted female, alternative woman, woman on the road

30 LILY: Peaceful decision, private road, retirement planning, old decision, making a discrete choice, making a mature decision, discreet separation, snowy road, restrained choice

31 SUN: Great possibility, good plan, good alternative, positive decision, courageous decision, fabulous choice, bright option, sunny path, golden opportunity, conscious decision, vacation planning

32 MOON: Emotional decision, off the beaten path, magickal path, creative option, intuitive choice, intuition guides your choice, influenced decision, recognizing possibilities, moonlit path

33 KEY: Open road, significant decision, karmic path, freedom of choice, open plan, important decision, fated decision, key decision, revealing options, noble choice, open to new ways, pivotal decision

34 FISH: Money decision, business plan, investment plan, budget, shopping options, financial decision, fluctuating decision, financial planning

35 ANCHOR: Long-term planning, down the road, weighty decision, secured options, weighing pros and cons, heavy indecision, stable plan, stuck between multiple options

36 CROSS: Difficult choice, very tough separation, at the crossroads, difficult plan, tough decision, multiple disappointments, regretting a decision, ethical choice, burdened by a decision, painful decision, religious decision, shameful choice

Sometimes we can choose the paths we follow. Sometimes our choices are made for us. And sometimes we have no choice at all.
—Neil Gaiman

23 Mice

Nibbling little by little, I take tiny pieces away
Spoiling everything good, bringing worries every day
Ruin happens gradually, you must pay attention
These costly things happen that nobody will mention

KEYWORDS

Diminished, Decay, Damage, Corrupt, Theft, Spoiled, Wearing down, Disintegrating, Infestation, Destruction, Fading, Vanishing, Lessening, Dirty, Ruined, Gnaws, Dwindling, Opportunistic, Depleted, Declining, Deteriorating, Repairs, Spread of disease, Costly (not money), Obsessive

MEANING

When the Mice come scurrying into your life, be vigilant because something is being nibbled away and being damaged bit by bit. And before you know, ruin will ensue and destroy anything in its wake.

Lenormand Mice Combinations

1 RIDER: Package stolen ("porch pirate"), news brings destruction, quick repair, drive is dwindling, news of damage, visitor steals something, quick and dirty, package lost, quickly fading

2 CLOVER: Luck's running out, opportunities diminish, chance disappearing, gambling costs you, gambling obsession, window of opportunity closing, game's lost

3 SHIP: Ship sinking, traveling less, taking the wind out of your sails, movement diminished, travel obsession, car theft, vehicle damage, car repairs

4 HOUSE: Home repairs, home invasion, property damage, family worries, real estate reduction, home robbery, house damage, home infestation

5 TREE: Fatigue, condition worsens, disease, hypochondriac, exhaustion, tooth decay, tree rot, health declines, patience wearing thin, vitality fades, fertility diminished

6 CLOUDS: Confusion subsides, doubting less, the storm weakens, depression lessens, troubles diminish, disturbances decrease, troubles vanish, hidden corruption

7 SNAKE: Problems, desire fades, lies spread, lies eating away at you, betrayal causes ruin, attraction weakens, enemies multiply, wire damage, pipe damage

8 COFFIN: Expiring, ending little by little, dying, deterioration, illness causes damage, loss, bad damage, decaying

9 BOUQUET: Occasion is ruined, beauty fades, party ruined, beauty obsession, invitation declined, art theft, flowers fade, surprise spoiled, gratitude diminishes, invitation lost

10 SCYTHE: Dangerously destructive, unexpected damage, sudden infestation, harvest spoiled, accidental damage, dangerous obsession, irrevocable damage

11 WHIP: Physically worn out (fatigue), arguments decrease, nagging, questionable theft, sexual obsession, disputing damages, investigating theft, anger

subsides, sex drive dwindles, rash of break-ins, compulsive obsession (OCD)

12 BIRDS: Conversation draining, phone call unsettling, feeling nervous, conversation fades, anxious and worried, talking dirty, negotiations ruined, anxiety wears you down, talking less

13 CHILD: Inexperience is costly, small repairs, innocence ruined, small obsession, new damage, vulnerable to theft, small infestation, little damage

14 FOX: Thick as thieves, suspecting corruption, faking a robbery, workplace theft, survival, working less, betrayal, stealthy observation, workaholic, job fatigue, scam causes damage

15 BEAR: Strength is weakening, big mess, power decreasing, big damage, foodie, diet stress, weight loss, food spoils, widespread, big worry

16 STARS: Online corruption, unclear, vision fading, exposing corruption, dreams diminished, inspiration fading, online theft

17 STORK: Restlessness, progress ruined, moving damage, change causes worry, cycle of corruption, seasonal damage, season fades

18 DOG: Friendship is draining, loyalty strained, pack behavior, dog obsession, friendship fades, watch for theft, support diminishes, I smell a rat!

19 TOWER: Corporate theft, incarceration, building crumbles, government corruption, opportunistic, self-sabotage, self-serving, official damage, ambition fades, loneliness dissipates, prison, tradition lost

20 GARDEN: Group mind, your network, event is ruined, crowded, the collective, teamwork diminishes, everybody, (online) group is damaging

21 MOUNTAIN: Restrictions lessened, barriers removed, obstacles diminishing, mountain crumbles, obstacles destroyed, climbing bit by bit, delays subside, limits reduced, distance lessens, permanent damage

22 PATHS: The process of elimination, path narrows, possibility diminishes, highway robbery, separation costly, decision gnaws you, multiple repairs, road to destruction, unusual robbery, being on the road wears you down

24 HEART: Passionless, love diminishes, relationship ruined, followers decline, attraction fades, disheartened, romance destroyed

25 RING: Contract dissolved, deal is corrupt, promises fade, marriage ruined, continual repairs, ring tarnishes, promises vanish, contract is flawed, agreement is worrisome, marriage is wearing you down

26 BOOK: Secrets are costly, information is corrupt, studying wears you out, knowledge wasted, secrets exposed little by little, education plummets, manuscript is destroyed, pages are ruined, unknown damage, memories fade

27 LETTER: Communicating less, messages eat away at you, text messages decrease, blackmail, messages vanishes, schedule is ruined, files are corrupted, results are damaging

28 MAN: Worried man, dirty man, lesser man, damaged man, corrupt man, stressed man, opportunistic man, draining man, ruined man, obsessive man

29 WOMAN: Worried female, dirty woman, spoiled woman, degraded woman, damaged lady, corrupt woman, stressed female, opportunistic woman, draining woman, ruined lady, obsessive female, lady is a shrew

30 LILY: Aging, retirement worries, peace destroyed, spoiled, ruined, expired, rotting, old and decaying, old damage, winter repairs, peace destroyed, ancient ruins

31 SUN: Throwing shade, daylight is fading, three blind mice, daily worries, sun damage, success wears you out, illuminating corruption, truth gnaws at you, vacationing less

32 MOON: Emotional decline, realizing the damage, intuition weakens, feeling depleted, nighttime robbery, creativity fades, reflecting on the damage caused, feeling stressed

33 KEY: Significant damage caused, access is decreased, revealing major sabotage, freedom is costly, new way is found, pay attention!

34 FISH: Funds deplete, alcohol impairment, financial stress, business is sabotaged, business robbery, business is dissolved, resources diminished, financial ruin, water subsides, financially draining, business worries

35 ANCHOR: Serious worries, persistent fatigue, heavy damage, steady decline, unstable, hold is lessening, routine repairs

36 CROSS: Consumed by worry, panic, critical damage, victim of theft, spirit vanishes, obligations wear you out, painful decline, faith destroyed, suffering ruin, major exhaustion

Building a better mousetrap merely results in smarter mice.
—Benjamin Franklin

24 Heart

The moment our eyes met is the moment I knew
My heart found a home, and I found it in you
You gave me your essence, and I sang to your soul
The two of us entwined, as my heart became whole

KEYWORDS

Love, Heartfelt, Passion, Romance, Relationship, the Heart, Compassion, Lover, Pleasure, Flirting, Kindness, Loving, Generosity, Affection, Dating, Forgiveness, Affairs of the heart, Philanthropy

MEANING

The Heart can represent all kinds of love, most commonly the romantic kind. It pulls at your heart strings guiding you to find your Heart's desire.

Lenormand Heart Combinations

1 RIDER: The Other Man, lover, suitor falls in love, potential relationship, declaration of love, news delivered compassionately

2 CLOVER: Lucky in love, short-term love affair, easy relationship, quick to fall in love, casual lover, taking a chance on love, whirlwind love affair, casually dating, opportunity for love, lighthearted, dalliance, casual relationship

3 SHIP: Foreign lover, long-distance relationship, longing, overseas lover, leaving a relationship, saying goodbye to a lover, navigating a relationship, sea of love

4 HOUSE: Home is where the heart is, family love, family relation, comfortable relationship, domestic affairs, family relationship

5 TREE: Healthy heart, growing adoration, spiritual kind of love, healthful relationship, ancestral love, deeply rooted relationship

6 CLOUDS: Sad romance, misunderstanding in the relationship, turbulent relationship, hiding a lover, hidden relationship, unclear intentions, confusing relationship, vague relationship

7 SNAKE: Dishonest relationship, jealous lover, complicated relationship ("it's complicated"), lying lover, betrayed in love, cheating heart, betrayal, illicit affair, affairs of the heart, cheating in a relationship, toxic love, lying about an attraction, cold hearted, toxic relationship

8 COFFIN: Bad romance, ending a relationship, ends in heartache, widow maker (heart condition), died of a broken heart, nonexistent relationship, bad date, closed heart, no passion, negative lover

9 BOUQUET: Beautiful relationship, generous heart, blissfully in love, blossoming romance, sweet love, roses, invited on a date, gift of love, attractive lover, beautiful heart, flaunting a relationship, generous lover

10 SCYTHE: A breakup, breaking a date, a broken heart, scared in love, divided love, a dangerous lover, cutting off a lover, accidentally falling in love, unexpected relationship, a risky relationship

11 WHIP: Sexual relationship, eroticism, BDSM-type relationship, critical lover, questionable relationship, abusive relationship, serial dater, fighting with a lover, aggressive lover

12 BIRDS: Words of love, conversations are flirtatious, flutters in your heart (butterflies), sweethearts, lovers, passionate discussions, whispering sweet nothings, anxious lover, listen to your heart, gossiping ardently, discussions about love and relationships, talking to a lover

13 CHILD: Young love, childhood sweetheart, short relationship, immature lover, vulnerable relationship, flirting, new relationship, childcare, first love

14 FOX: Work relationship, working on a relationship, sneaky lover, workplace flirting, fake relationship, guilty heart, office romance, stolen heart, passionate about your job, taking advantage of kindness, guilty pleasure, a catfish

15 BEAR: Dominant lover, huge heart, overbearing lover, big love, boss with a big heart, power of love, determined lover, boldly flirting, strong relationship, forced relationship

16 STARS: Falling in love, dream lover, promising relationship, online dating, greatest love story, celebrity crush, like a star, wishing for love, eternal love, blessed relationship, exposing the relationship, defining the relationship, high-profile romance

17 STORK: Taking the next step, change of heart, reentering the dating scene, relocating for love, restless heart, progressive relationship, returning lover, changes in the relationship

18 DOG: Platonic relationship, friends in love, unconditional love, guarding your heart, loyal lover, protective lover, friendly romance, familiar lover, friends to lovers, reliable relationship, supportive lover

19 TOWER: Jilted lover, past relationship, officially dating, established relationship, lonely heart, lonely in a relationship, past relationship, past lover, prisoner of love, arrogant lover, official relationship

20 GARDEN: Playing the field, meeting a lover, group date, uncommitted lover, a player, polyamory (multiple lovers), uncommitted relationship, dating, PDA (public display of affection)

21 MOUNTAIN: Blocked romance, obstacle in the relationship, indifferent lover, lack of fulfillment, blocked heart, stubborn love, challenging relationship, tough love, hardened heart, rough lover

22 PATHS: Parting ways, multiple partners, alternative relationship, romantic options, wanderlust, choosing between lovers, decision about love, possibility of romance, many paths to love, multiple lovers, multiple dates

23 MICE: Damaged relationship, deteriorating relationship, tainted love, fading love, worried about a relationship, less affection, obsessive lover, fewer likes (social-media "hearts")

25 RING: Marriage proposal, wedding band, married, engaged, partnership, promise of love, bound by love, vow of love, committed relationship, married love, common-law

26 BOOK: Secret relationship, secret lover, secret admirer, book of love, researching a lover, remembering a great love, relationship journal, passionate about learning

27 LETTER: Sending a message of love, texting a lover, message from a lover, writing love letters, romantic message, posting an ad to find love, sending love, blogging about love and relationships, message of love

28 MAN: Male lover, passionate man, generous man, heart-shaped-face man, big-hearted man, gentleman, considerate man, kindhearted man, compassionate man, philanthropist

29 WOMAN: Female lover, passionate woman, generous woman, heart-shaped-face woman, big-hearted female, gentlewoman, considerate woman, tender woman, kind lady, compassionate woman, philanthropist

30 LILY: Old flame, experienced lover, mature lover, older lover, cold hearted, established relationship, discreet lover, private relationship

31 SUN: Thriving relationship, true love, happily in love, joyful love, burning love, good heart, bright romantic forecast, good relationship, summer love, hot lover, true generosity, warm heart, renewed romance, truthful lover, holiday romance

32 MOON: Crazy kind of love, skillful lover, feeling loved, great affection, emotional intimacy, creative passion, reflecting on a relationship, intuitive lover

33 KEY: Open relationship, open your heart, YES to love, key relationship, important romance, open to love, soulful kinda love, karmic love, significant relationship, destined romance, fated love, noble heart, freedom to love

34 FISH: Deep affection, business relationship, cash donation, wealthy lover, letting passion flow, dating ("plenty of fish"), sugar daddy, sugar mama, deep love, investing in a relationship, transactional relationship

35 ANCHOR: Steady romance, serious relationship, settling down, long-term relationship, feeling tied down, stable relationship, long-lasting love, solid relationship, stuck in a relationship

36 CROSS: Obligatory relationship, testing your lover, ashamed of the relationship, gave up on love, painful relationship, being a martyr in love, suffering in a relationship, disappointing relationship, difficult partner, having faith in your lover, regretting a relationship

So, I love you because the entire universe conspired to help me find you. —Paulo Coelho

25 Ring

Give me your hand, my maiden fair
For I will put a golden ring on there
Bound by oath, with this ring I do wed
Till death do us part, the Bridegroom said

KEYWORDS

Commitments, Agreements, Unions, Circle, Connections, Engagements, Marriage, Continual, Jewelry, Contracts, Deals, Round, Promise, Bonds, Proposal, Circulation, Vows, Inner circle, Dedicated, Offer

MEANING

The Ring card represents all types of commitments and agreements; look to the cards next to the Ring to discern the theme. The shape of the Ring is also significant, for it speaks of cycles and circles or anything that is continual in nature.

Lenormand Ring Combinations

1 RIDER: News of an agreement, delivering the contract, quick deal, announcing the banns, news about a deal, news is circulating, Other Man is married, moving around in circles, announcing an offer

2 CLOVER: Short-term agreement, fortunate deal, lucky contract, casual wedding, informal agreement, surprise engagement, easy connection, casual offer

3 SHIP: International contract, foreign agreement, travel deal, overseas wedding, car lease, shipping contract, travel arrangements, exploring connections, trade agreement, destination wedding, travel contract

4 HOUSE: Lease agreement, family connections, brand deal, family bond, real estate deal, real estate offer, family circle (family bubble)

5 TREE: Stable contract, healing circle, treatment is ongoing, spiritual circle, healthy marriage, spiritual contract, growing connection, extending an offer, spiritual connection

6 CLOUDS: Confusing contract, uncertain promise, vague deal, sad marriage, unclear agreement, misunderstanding a connection, troubled marriage, hidden agreement, confusing offer

7 SNAKE: Lies continue, desiring commitment, betraying your partner, self-serving agreement, adultery, wanting a connection, problems in paradise, lying on a contract, crooked deal, toxic marriage, infidelity continues, complex offer

8 COFFIN: Ending a marriage, lost ring, losing a deal, rescind an offer, ending a commitment, done deal, calling off an engagement, canceled contract, silent agreement, final offer, void agreement, bad deal, empty promise, no deal, bad marriage, death of a spouse

9 BOUQUET: Happy marriage, beautiful union, presenting an offer, fair deal, social engagement, event contract, favorable agreement, pleasing contract, gift of jewelry, sweet deal

10 SCYTHE: Divorce, breach of contract, broken promises, breaking a contract, broken ring, breaking a cycle, risky deal, removing a ring, irrevocable agreement, broken marriage, divorce agreement

11 WHIP: Disputing a contract, vicious circle, competing for a contract, questionable marriage, repeated promises, sexual agreement, sexual-consent contract, striking a deal, a sex ring, sexual proposition, disagreement

12 BIRDS: Rumors circulating, negotiating a deal, nervous about commitment, partnership agreement, verbal agreement, nervous about proposing, verbal commitment, music deal, discussing a contract, gossip going around

13 CHILD: New agreement, adoption agreement, short engagement, small promise, new connection, newlyweds, small deal, simple contract, new deal

14 FOX: Suspicious contract, working on a marriage, manipulating a contract, insincere promise, sneaky deal, fake contract, work contract, false agreement, fake ring, reneged on an agreement

15 BEAR: Strong marriage, forced agreement, powerful bond, big deal, huge commitment, big promise, strong offer

16 STARS: Future marriage, diamond ring, hoping for marriage, wishing for engagement, connection, straightforward contract, inspirational connection, stellar deal, clear commitment, eternity band, high-profile marriage, online offer

17 STORK: Return, moving continuously, changed agreement, going around in circles, seasonal contract, comeback, modifying a contract, progressive marriage, moving contract, turn around

18 DOG: Faithful marriage, loyal bond, friendly promise, helpful connection, friendly agreement, dog collar, support continues, very dedicated

19 TOWER: Corporate merger, legal agreement, firm deal, official engagement, handcuffs, traditional wedding, prior connection, legal marriage, rules of engagement, government contract, lonely in marriage, enforcing a contract, defending a marriage

20 GARDEN: Club, garden wedding, outdoor wedding, landscaping contract, public engagement, public promise, social circle (social bubble), members' ring, group deal, club contract

21 MOUNTAIN: Inner circle, boundaries, permanent agreement, challenging a contract, hard deal, remote connection, difficult commitment, delayed promise, challenging marriage

22 PATHS: Separation, multiple marriages, separation agreement, countless promises, polygamy, alternative marriage, the pros and cons of a deal, path goes around in circles, unusual deal, multiple offers

23 MICE: Stolen ring, dissolving a marriage, stolen contract, crumbling marriage, lessening bond, collective agreement, declining an offer, failing marriage, messy offer

24 HEART: Heartfelt commitment, loving union, special bond, relationship contract, love connection, generous deal, flirting with commitment, wholehearted promise, loving marriage

26 BOOK: Secret agreement, educational proposal, secret deal, mysterious connection, book deal, publishing contract, book proposal, secret promise, book dedication, unknown connection, research proposal

27 LETTER: Written agreement, penned contract, marriage certificate, written promise, emailed contract, writing vows, writing a proposal, newspaper circulation, written agreement

28 MAN: Committed man, husband, married man, taken man, honorable man, partner, connected man, dedicated man, round-faced man

29 WOMAN: Committed woman, wife, married woman, devoted woman, taken woman, partner, connected woman, dedicated lady, round-faced woman

30 LILY: Long-term agreement, old agreement, discreet agreement, old promise, long commitment, retirement agreement, old contract, private deal

31 SUN: Successful marriage, shiny gold ring, happy union, golden handcuffs, successful deal, happily married, successful contract, good offer, renewing vows, happily ever after, rewarding deal

32 MOON: Emotional bond, emotional commitment, intuitive connection, full-moon circle, binding spell, coven, creative offer, psychic circle, full moon

33 KEY: Important agreement, open agreement, a way out of a contract, open marriage, noble promise, swearing an oath, important deal, karmic/soul connection, access to the inner circle, a way out of the marriage

34 FISH: Business agreement, prenuptial agreement, business proposal, financial partnership, prosperous deal, financial agreement, exchanging a ring, water circulating, investment proposal

35 ANCHOR: Secure agreement, serious commitment, fixed contract, long-lasting marriage, solid deal, routine contract, long-term agreement

36 CROSS: Obligated by a promise, binding contract, prayer circle, painful union, burdened by a promise, critical agreement, faith circle, a spirit circle, sacred vow, an offering, regretting a commitment, difficult deal, disappointing marriage

One Ring to rule them all, One Ring to find them,
One Ring to bring them all, and in the darkness bind them.
—J. R. R. Tolkien, The Lord of the Rings

26 Book

Pages turning ever so gently, the lives many encased inside
Secrets guarded very closely, skeletons you choose to hide
Information shrouded in mystery, many stories yet untold
A Book is a source of knowledge, the greatest gift to behold

KEYWORDS

Secrets, a Book, Information, Knowledge, Wisdom, Manuscript, Facts, Journal, Diary, Unknown, Expert, History, Education, Studies, Memories, Research, Learning, Lesson, Training

MEANING

The main theme of the Book is secrets. The Book highlights anything involving formal education, information, studies, research, knowledge, and academic learning.

Lenormand Book Combinations

1 RIDER: Incoming information, arrival unknown, receiving quick information, riding expert, visitor information, actively learning, student, first-edition book

2 CLOVER: Comic book, lucky information, brief history, gambling expert, fleeting memory, lucky knowledge, exciting information, surprising secret, funny memory, lucky lesson

3 SHIP: Long-distance learning, exploration, journey into the unknown, foreign studies, travel book, destination unknown, travel expert, travel journal, ship's logbook

4 HOUSE: Real estate expert, family secrets, homework, family history, scrapbook, family album, home library, inside information, homeschooling, the house has a secret, family memories

5 TREE: Medical journal, health information, growing knowledge, medical mystery, spiritual knowledge, wisdom, health research, medical expert, ancestral memories, blood memory, vital information, spiritual studies, life lesson, health history, spiritual lesson, medical training, med school

6 CLOUDS: Confusion, unknown, shrouded in mystery, hidden secrets, ignorance, vague memories, hidden information, mental health expert, muddled logic, misunderstanding the information, dark secret, doubtful information, hidden knowledge, disturbing secret

7 SNAKE: Lying about knowing any information, betraying a secret, wanting more information, transformative information, complicated history, deceptive information

8 COFFIN: Keeping a secret, dropping out of school, outcome unknown, skeleton in the closet, buried secrets, death is mysterious, funeral memory book, grief expert, bad secret, cause of death unknown, closed book, end of training

9 BOUQUET: Beauty expert, art portfolio, surprising information, beauty secrets, blossoming knowledge, gratitude journal, gift of knowledge, beautiful memory, art classes, design school

10 SCYTHE: Dangerous information, hurtful secret, dangerous knowledge, sudden information, cutting class, accidental information, dropping out of school, accelerated classes, gathering information

11 WHIP: Questioning information, sexual history, erotic magazine, sex expert, abusing information, sexual secret, erotic novel, difficulty keeping a secret, sex education, sexual memory

12 BIRDS: Lecture, telephone book, audio book, telling secrets ("spilling the tea"), gossiping about secrets, small lessons, a conversation about education, songbook, little training, nervous about a secret, remembering a conversation

13 CHILD: New book, elementary school, childhood memories, childhood secret, small secret, vulnerable information, elementary student, new information, child expert, children's book

14 FOX: Suspicious information, on-the-job training, misinformation, work secret, false information, a professional, a workbook, misleading information, employment history, manipulating information

15 BEAR: Big secret, diet research, food journal, a cookbook, foodie, powerful information, diet history, overbearing information, strong learner, big lesson, weight training

16 STARS: Bestseller, online classes, award-winning book, e-book, positive memories, higher education, social-media expert, night school, online research, influential book, invaluable lesson, online training, astrology book, sci-fi novel, online school

17 STORK: Moving away for school, transferring schools, changing results, exchange student, changing courses, birth classes, switching classes, returning to school

18 DOG: Friend's secret, dependable research, guarding secrets, reliable information, dog breed research, looking for information, help with research, classmate, guidebook, reliable training, police academy, military training

19 TOWER: Formal education, rule book, legal expert, "by the book," ancient history, established education, past history, operations manual, company handbook, corporate secrets, law books, law school, self-serving information, formal training, past memories, history book

20 GARDEN: Public classes, public library, public knowledge, group learning, public information, common knowledge, shared secret, common sense, gardening expert, group training

21 MOUNTAIN: Remote learning, delaying studies, hard training, climbing expert, restricted information, stalled research, delayed manuscript, obstacles unknown, interrupted education, distance education, hard lesson

22 PATHS: Multiple degrees, many secrets, choosing your courses, unusual book, many books, double major, choice of schools, alternative education, the path is unknown, street smarts, many lessons learned

23 MICE: Stressed about school, dirty secret, worried about secrets, many memories, many books, burned out by studying, destroying information, costly secret, stealing books, collective knowledge, damaging information, damaged book, stressful training

24 HEART: Romance novel, dating history, intimate secret, fond memories, relationship expert, relationship secret, love of learning

25 RING: Sworn to secrecy, continuing education, marital secrets, contract information, marriage expert, continuous training, well-rounded knowledge

27 LETTER: Diploma, a writer, university application, writing in a diary, thesis, dissertation, transcript, degree, report card, message containing secrets, writing a book

28 MAN: Secretive man, educated man, mysterious man, unknown man, intelligent man, author, academic, male student, male teacher, professor

29 WOMAN: Secretive woman, educated woman, mysterious lady, unknown female, intelligent woman, author, academic, female student, female teacher, professor

30 LILY: Private information, old lesson, "old school," old book, wisdom, lifelong learning, private school, mature student, history book, life experience, old secret, reminiscing

31 SUN: Day school, enlightening knowledge, true story, daily information, conscious knowledge, good memories, good secret, truthful information, successful student, summer school, successful training, good lesson, good book

32 MOON: Night school, occult studies, art school, psychology studies, paranormal novel, fantasy novel, dream journal, feelings are unknown, emotional intelligence, psychic training

33 KEY: Significant information, noteworthy manuscript, open book, prestigious school, acclaimed book, revealing secrets, important knowledge, karmic knowledge, key information, important book, karmic lesson, important training

34 FISH: Business secret, scholarship, financial secrets, royalties, financial literacy, bank book, financial information, finance expert, business school, business information, business guru, financial history, financial lesson

35 ANCHOR: Heavy secrets, marine expert, sound information, solid education, stable knowledge, consistent information, solid history, routine training

36 CROSS: Burdened by secrets, tests, exams, regret keeping secrets, religious books, religious expert, Catholic school, shameful secret, burned out by studying, disappointing information, painful memories, difficult education, devotional book, difficult lesson

I owe everything I am and everything I will ever be to books.
—Gary Paulsen

27 Letter

A handwritten letter, a cherished memento I keep
Surviving the test of time, a memory felt so deep
Emails and texts will fade, getting deleted over time
A letter penned by your hand is a gift so sublime

KEYWORDS

Letter, Something written, Emails, Texts, Communication, Schedule, Cards, Mail, Certificate, Notes, Writer, Results, Documents, Files, Papers, Messages, Newspaper, Advertisement, Poster, Brochures, Blog, Lists, Sending, a Review, a Post

MEANING

The Letter is a card all about communication and the written word. Updated meaning includes any electronic "typed" communication such as texts, emails, and posts.

Lenormand Letter Combinations

1 RIDER: Incoming text message, broadcast, newsletter, delivered message, newspaper, quick message, news-feed story, fast results

2 CLOVER: Lottery ticket, brief message, cheerful note, deck of cards, bucket list, exciting email, quick text, wagering ticket, comedy writer, informal results

3 SHIP: Foreign document, travel card, driver's license, travel post, passport, travel documents, boarding pass, travel visa, air mail, travel review, foreign correspondence, travel itinerary, travel blog, map, goodbye letter, DM (direct message)

4 HOUSE: Real estate documents, property deed, real estate listing, real estate post, family documents, family newsletter, real estate brochure, home page, mortgage papers, real estate blog

5 TREE: Prescription, medical chart, spiritual message, medical referral, medical file, DNA results, spiritual blog, medical results, medical documents, health requisition, ancestral documents, lab results, health-and-wellness blog

6 CLOUDS: Vague messages, confusing texts, hidden messages, depressing letter, sad texts, confusing post, obscured messages, upsetting message, disappointing results, cloud documents, disturbing message, confusing communications

7 SNAKE: Envious message, seductive texts, "poison pen" letter, jealous texts, deceptive messages, cheating text, complicated message, toxic communication, problems with email, betraying text messages

8 COFFIN: Final notice, letter of resignation, blackmail, negative result, deleted messages, bad message, condolence card, a will, suicide note, death certificate, final message, negative email, bad review, final draft, ending communication, "naughty list," terrible results

9 BOUQUET: Invitation, pleasant email, wonderful review, presenting a letter, gift registry, thank-you card, beautiful message, art of writing letters, guest list, amazing results

10 SCYTHE: Wounding letter, cutting off communications, vaccine passport, vaccine certificate, risky communications, blunt message, risky post, divorce papers, unexpected message, autumn schedule

11 WHIP: Angry message, inconclusive results, abusive texts, sexting, sexual post, spam email, angry review, sexual messages, erotic letters, back-and-forth messaging, a sex blog

12 BIRDS: Voicemail, airline ticket, tweet, talk to text, gossip column, talking, songwriting, music blog, flight itinerary

13 CHILD: Short message, immature text, new post, playful texts, new message, playing cards, vulnerable letter, inexperienced writer, underestimating a message

14 FOX: Untrustworthy results, work communication, misleading resume, scam email, work email, wrong text sent, fake review, work newsletter, fraudulent documents, suspicious texts, work schedule, manipulating results, fake post, forged signature

15 BEAR: Strong email, powerful message, recipe, shopping list, grocery flyer, forced communication, aggressive message, food log, restaurant review, food blog

16 STARS: Hopeful message, positive result, astrology chart, inspirational blog, fan page, positive review, digital photos, vision board, inspiring message, clear message, inspirational post, horoscope, fan mail, famous writer, motivational message

17 STORK: Changing results, birth certificate, forwarded message, birthday card, changing schedule, long message, pregnancy results, seasonal newsletter, rescheduling, return to sender, spring schedule

18 DOG: Reliable communication, trust the results, dog blog, friendly message, helpful email, on a friend's page, helpful review, loyalty card, supportive messages, friendly text

19 TOWER: Legal documents, official document, official review, establishing communication, official letter, legal notice, formal letter, voting ballot (card), registered mail

20 GARDEN: Public message, public notice, group text, public documents, public post, network message, public schedule, group email, public report, group text, public review, meeting minutes, group message, group schedule, meeting agenda, gardening blog

21 MOUNTAIN: Delayed message, harsh review, blocked posts, rough text, customs documents, blocked messages, blocked emails, grueling schedule

22 PATHS: Multiple messages, many documents, many files, unusual communication, multiple posts, pros-and-cons list, numerous emails, several texts, a decision in writing, separation documents

23 MICE: Obsessive messages, corrupted files, diminished messages, stressful communication, stealing mail, distressing texts, corrupted email, stolen post, dirty text, damaging message, plagiarizing

24 HEART: Love letter, passionate message, heartfelt text, flirty text, love note, sweet message, lovely review, Valentine's card, loving the results, romantic text, relationship blog, heartfelt message, kind note, passionate letter

25 RING: Conclusive results, marriage certificate, binding document, circulating email, chain letter, binding document, offer letter, marriage blog

26 BOOK: Report card, school newsletter, diploma, published paper, book review, mysterious message, informative email, educational documents, research paper, secret ballot, secret message, writer's blog, book signing

28 MAN: Expressive man, blogger, writer, message from a man, composed man, eloquent man, communicative man, thoughtful man, sentimental man

29 WOMAN: Expressive woman, blogger, writer, message from a woman, composed lady, eloquent lady, communicative woman, thoughtful woman, sentimental woman

30 LILY: Old messages, antique papers, private blog, cold text, winter schedule, private message, private post, retirement blog, old review, winter schedule

31 SUN: Good results, sunshine letter, annual newsletter, "nice list," daily blog, warm message, summertime schedule, good review, warm message, truthful message, happy email, successful blog, good message, winning ticket, good communication

32 MOON: Tarot cards, oracle cards, Lenormand cards, emotional message, creative blog, intuitive message, manifesting results, paranormal writer, fantasy writer, automatic writing, talented writer

33 KEY: Important document, open communications, significant message, open ticket, a key card, revealing message, important email, pass card, destined to write, esteemed author, important message

34 FISH: Business letter, bank statement, phishing email, money, checks, business files, invoice, IOU note, business review, business documents, pay stub, business license, credit card, financial statements, money blog

35 ANCHOR: Saved messages or letters, safe communication, serious message, navel chart, routine post, standard email, persistent texts, routine email, regular schedule, holding on to a letter

36 CROSS: Painful results, to-do list, critical message, Spirit or Ouija board, regretting a message sent, religious pamphlet, tough message, disappointing message, difficult schedule, burdensome emails, obligatory email, test results, painful story, religious blog

> *More than kisses, letters mingle souls.*
> *—John Donne*

PLEASE NOTE: Next you will meet the Man and Woman cards. These two belong to a very old system from days of yore, before the days of freedom to express yourself in the way you choose, and live how you want to live, and love whom you want to love. Feel free to adapt these cards in the way of your choosing and assign any meaning you choose. Even if you choose to be a unicorn!

Mossy green eyes penetrating, giving a smoldering look
A mysterious air about him, secretive like a closed book
Masculine energy oozing, drenched in intoxicating desire
Making my heart skip a beat and setting my soul on fire

KEYWORDS

The Querent, a Man known to the Querent, a Male significant other, a Man, a Gentleman, a Male significator, a Male family member, a Male, a Husband, a Fiancée, a Partner, a Boyfriend, a Male friend, Everyman, Masculine energy, Male influence, a Boy

MEANING

When the Man card steps into your life, it represents an actual person. If the Seeker is male it represents him; if the Seeker is of the opposite sex, it would represent an important male or a known man in their life.

Lenormand Man Combinations

1 RIDER: Flamboyant man, male visitor or caller, man arrives, the Other Man, news about a man, male suitor, attractive young man

2 CLOVER: The gambler, lucky man, risk-taker, Irish man, casual man, happy-go-lucky man, lighthearted man, funny man, exciting man

3 SHIP: Foreign man, male traveler, worldly man, vagabond, ship's captain, male gypsy, jet-setter, male that works in travel and tourism

4 HOUSE: Family man, man of the house, male family member, male relative, man with strong family values, lord of the manor, homeowner, homeboy, handyman

5 TREE: Shaman, patient man, spiritual man, healthy man, male ancestor, physician, medicine man, male linage, natural man, virile man

6 CLOUDS: Confused man, sad man, moody man, troubled man, depressed man, unstable man, shady man, anarchist, man full of doubt, "that man is trouble!"

7 SNAKE: Seductive man, dishonest man, cheating man, male enemy, toxic man, jealous man, charming man ("snake charmer"), deceptive man, mean man ("mean like a snake"), Prince Charming, snake oil salesman

8 COFFIN: Negative man, grieving man, widow, empty man, unlucky man, bad man, dying man, closed-off man, deceased male, silent man, a dead man, burdensome man

9. BOUQUET: Social man, handsome man, conceited man, delightful man, wonderful man, considerate man, artistic man, flashy man, grateful man, sweet man, pleasant man, poetic man, polite man

10 SCYTHE: Impulsive man, hurtful man, an ex, ruthless man, dangerous man, decisive man, broken man, cutting off a man, severing ties with a man, divorced man

11 WHIP: Aggressive man, argumentative man, abusive man, sexual man, a dominant, violent man, kinky man, abused man, creature of habit, active man, sexy man, competitive man, personal trainer

12 BIRDS: Talkative man, nervous man, restless man, vocal man, curious male, male singer, male musician, pilot, flight attendant, gossiping man, brother, anxious man, two men

13 CHILD: Young man, vulnerable man, immature man, new man, small man, innocent man, short man, naive man, man-child, playful man, inexperienced man, slight man, a boy

14 FOX: Cunning man, sly man, red-haired man, con man, sneaky man, manipulative man, shallow man, guilty man, male coworker, male employee, working man

15 BEAR: Powerful man, dominant man, forceful man, obese man, bearded man, boss man, overbearing man, muscular man, large man, big man, overweight man, hairy man, strong man

16 STARS: Famous man, male influencer, inspiring man, hopeful man, positive man, goal-oriented man, dreamer, visionary, optimistic man, good-natured man, man of your dreams, philosophical man

17 STORK: A man returns, tall man, transitioning male, evolved man, sophisticated man, monogamous man, quiet man, caring man, graceful man, progressive man, restless man

18 DOG: Faithful man, submissive man, friendly man, helpful man, loyal man, dependable man, trustworthy man, familiar man, male friend, supportive man, policeman

19 TOWER: Ambitious man, traditional man, man from the past, egotistical man, arrogant man, lonely man, proud man, imposing man, formal man, established man, controlling man

20 GARDEN: A player, male public figure, popular man, single man, playboy, cultured man, country boy, boy's club, uncommitted man, men in general, group of men, available man

21 MOUNTAIN: Stubborn man, hard man, distant man, indifferent man, hostile man, rugged man, challenging man, mountain man, unavailable man, hard-to-reach man

22 PATHS: Indecisive man, separated man, unfamiliar man, multiple men, unusual man, two-timing man, uncommitted man, alternative man, man on the road

23 MICE: Worried man, dirty man, lesser man, damaged man, corrupt man, stressed man, opportunistic man, draining man, ruined man, obsessive man

24 HEART: Male lover, passionate man, generous man, heart-shaped-face man, big-hearted man, gentleman, considerate man, kindhearted man, compassionate man, philanthropist

25 RING: Committed man, husband, married man, taken man, honorable man, partner, connected man, dedicated man, round-faced man

26 BOOK: Secretive man, educated man, mysterious man, unknown man, intelligent man, author, academic, male student, male teacher, professor

27 LETTER: Expressive man, blogger, writer, message from a man, composed man, eloquent man, communicative man, thoughtful man, sentimental man

29 WOMEN: *See Woman card for combinations; when the Woman card shows up, it's literally a woman

30 LILY: Father, father figure, grandfather, older man, experienced man, wise man, "silver fox," private man, pensioner, calm man, mature man, retired man, cold man, discrete man

31 SUN: Masculine, successful man, warm man, energetic man, optimistic man, courageous man, good man, confident man, truthful man, male energy

32 MOON: Creative man, emotional man, intuitive man, talented man, moon-faced man, compelling man, fantasy man, sensitive man, male witch, skillful man, man on the moon

33 KEY: Free man, important man, soulmate, distinguished man, significant man, open man, influential man, noble man, key man, honorable man, available man, sophisticated man, nobleman, dignified man

34 FISH: Materialistic man, businessman, entrepreneur, money man, wealthy man, independent man, man with deep pockets, alcoholic, investor, resourceful man

35 ANCHOR: Stable man, settled man, serious man, persistent man, safe man, secure man, grounded man, solid man, stuck man

36 CROSS: Religious man, miserable man, tormented man, defeated man, afflicted man, needy man, painful man, obligated man, suffering man, burdened man, remorseful man, difficult man, disappointing man, man in crisis, exhausted man, male spirit

You have to be a man before you can be a gentleman.
—John Wayne

29 Woman

Woman so strong, dare you underestimate me?
I cannot be possessed, I will always be free
Sovereign of my nation, I grant you your leave
Want to know my secret? It's the power to believe

KEYWORDS

The Querent, a Woman known to the Querent, a Woman, a Female significant other, a Lady, a Female significator, a Female family member, a Female, a Wife, a Fiancée, a Partner, a Girlfriend, a Female friend, Everywoman, Feminine energy, Female influence, a Girl

MEANING

When the Woman card steps into your life, it represents an actual person. If the Seeker is female it represents her; if the Seeker is the opposite sex, it would represent an important female or a known woman in their life.

Lenormand Woman Combinations

1 RIDER: Colorful lady, woman visitor or caller, woman arrives, news about a lady, female admirer, attractive young lady

2 CLOVER: Lady luck, gambling woman, risk-taker, Irish woman, casual woman, happy-go-lucky woman, lighthearted woman, funny lady, exciting woman

3 SHIP: Foreign woman, female traveler, international woman, ship's captain, female gypsy, jet-setter, bohemian, woman that works in travel and tourism

4 HOUSE: Nurturer, lady of the house, female family member, housekeeper, landlady, female relative, female with strong family values, lady of the manor, homeowner, homegirl

5 TREE: Healer, patient woman, spiritual woman, healthy woman, female ancestor, physician, medicine woman, female linage, natural woman, fruitful woman

6 CLOUDS: Confused lady, sad woman, moody woman, troubled lady, depressed woman, unstable woman, shady lady, rebellious woman, woman full of doubt, "that woman is trouble!"

7 SNAKE: Seductive female, dishonest woman, cheating female, female energy, toxic woman, jealous woman, female, striking lady, enemy, alluring woman, deceptive woman, mean woman, charlatan, sensual woman, the Other Woman, curvy woman

8 COFFIN: Negative woman, grieving lady, widow, empty woman, unlucky lady, bad woman, dying woman, closed-off female, deceased female, silent woman, burdensome woman

9 BOUQUET: Social butterfly, beautiful woman, fashionable woman, artistic woman, conceited woman, delightful woman, wonderful lady, considerate woman, fancy female, grateful lady, sweet woman, pleasant female, poetic female, polite woman

10 SCYTHE: Impulsive lady, hurtful woman, an ex, ruthless woman, dangerous female, decisive female, broken woman, cutting off a woman, securing ties with a female, divorced woman

11 WHIP: Aggressive woman, argumentative lady, abusive woman, sexual female, a dominatrix, feisty female, kinky female, abused woman, creature of habit, fierce woman, active female, sexy lady, competitive female, personal trainer

12 BIRDS: A bird, "Chatty Cathy," nervous lady, restless woman, vocal lady, curious female, female singer, female musician, pilot, flight attendant, gossiping woman, sister, anxious woman, two ladies

13 CHILD: Young lady, vulnerable woman, immature woman, new woman, petite lady, innocent woman, short woman, naive lady, playful woman, inexperienced female, timid woman, slight woman, a girl

14 FOX: Shrewd woman, sneaky female, red-haired woman, con artist, foxy lady, scheming woman, manipulative woman, guilty woman, female coworker, female employee, fake woman, superficial lady, working woman

15 BEAR: Mother, grandmother, mother figure, formidable woman, dominant lady, pushy lady, obese woman, boss lady, overbearing woman, a large woman, an overweight woman, strong woman

16 STARS: Famous woman, female influencer, inspiring female, hopeful woman, positive lady, goal-oriented woman, dreamer, visionary, optimistic woman, good-natured lady, dream girl, enlightened woman

17 STORK: Woman returns, tall woman, transitioning female, evolved woman, sophisticated lady, monogamous woman, quiet lady, caring woman, graceful lady, progressive woman, classy lady, restless woman

18 DOG: Faithful woman, known female, submissive female, friendly woman, helpful lady, loyal woman, dependable woman, trustworthy woman, familiar woman, female friend, supportive woman, policewoman

19 TOWER: Ambitious woman, traditional woman, woman from the past, selfish woman, haughty lady, lonely woman, intimidating woman, established woman, controlling woman

20 GARDEN: Femme fatale, female public figure, socialite, party girl, popular woman, country girl, single lady, women in general, cultured woman, group of ladies, woman's group, uncommitted female, available woman

21 MOUNTAIN: Stubborn woman, disinterested woman, harsh woman, distant woman, nonchalant female, hostile woman, challenging female, unavailable woman, hard-to-reach woman

22 PATHS: Indecisive lady, separated woman, unfamiliar lady, multiple women, unusual woman, two-timing woman, uncommitted female, alternative woman, woman on the road

23 MICE: Worried female, dirty woman, spoiled woman, degraded woman, damaged lady, corrupt woman, stressed female, opportunistic woman, draining woman, ruined lady, obsessive female, "the lady is a shrew"

24 HEART: Female lover, passionate woman, generous woman, heart-shaped-face woman, big-hearted female, gentlewoman, considerate woman, tender woman, kind lady, compassionate woman, philanthropist

25 RING: A committed woman, a wife, a married woman, a devoted woman, round-faced woman, a taken woman, an honorable lady, a partner, a connected woman, a dedicated lady

26 BOOK: Secretive woman, educated woman, mysterious lady, unknown female, intelligent woman, author, academic, female student, female teacher, professor

27 LETTER: Expressive woman, blogger, writer, message from a woman, composed lady, eloquent lady, communicative woman, thoughtful woman, sentimental woman

28 MAN: *See Man card for combinations; when the Man card shows up, it's literally a man

30 LILY: Older lady, experienced woman, wise woman, private woman, pensioner, peaceful lady, calm woman, mature woman, retired woman, cold woman, discreet lady, silver-haired lady

31 SUN: Successful woman, warm woman, energetic woman, optimistic lady, courageous woman, good woman, confident lady, truthful woman, female energy

32 MOON: Feminine, creative lady, emotional woman, intuitive woman, moon-faced woman, compelling woman, fantasy woman, sensitive woman, female witch, skillful woman

33 KEY: Regal woman, free woman, important woman, soulmate, unforgettable woman, significant female, influential lady, key female, honorable woman, available woman, sophisticated woman, dignified lady, prestigious woman, noblewoman

34 FISH: Material girl, businesswoman, entrepreneur, wealthy lady, independent woman, gold digger, woman with a big purse, alcoholic, investor, resourceful woman

35 ANCHOR: Stable woman, settled woman, persistent woman, safe woman, secure lady, grounded woman, solid woman, stuck woman

36 CROSS: Pious woman, miserable woman, tormented lady, defeated woman, remorseful woman, afflicted female, needy woman, pained woman, obligated woman, suffering female, burdened woman, difficult woman, disappointing woman, woman in crisis, worn-out woman, female spirit

Women who seek to be equal with men lack ambition.
—Marilyn Monroe

30 Lily

Lily white Flower, serene but so cold
Reminiscent of something, weathered and old
Matured with age, experience unrivaled
Discernment is key to the Lily's ongoing survival

KEYWORDS
Old, Mature, Aged, Calm, Wise, Discreet, Winter, Restrained, Father or grandfather, Discernment, Retirement, Experienced, Peaceful, Rest, Lasting a lifetime, Private, Cold, Ancient

MEANING
When the Lily card graces a spread, the meanings can be flexible and many. The most common way to read the Lily is as a card of age and maturity. With age comes life experience, and can denote someone's lifetime.

Lenormand Lily Combinations_

1 RIDER: News is calming, announcing retirement, mature young man, news about an older man, visiting senior, arrival of peace, active senior

2 CLOVER: Chance for peace, chance of a lifetime, semiretired, gambling senior, funny senior, happy retirement, lucky lifetime, carefree retirement, gambling restraint, chance for early retirement

3 SHIP: Journey north, snowbird, traveling seniors, navigating old age, foreign senior, trip of a lifetime

4 HOUSE: Father, grandfather, real estate experience, family discretion needed, house is showing its age, relative retires, living in the same house for a lifetime

5 TREE: Life experience, extremely slow, spiritually at peace, longevity, long rest period, healthy senior, ancestors, growing old, extending the olive branch

6 CLOUDS: Alzheimer's disease, senile, confused elder, cloud of snow, sad senior, depressed about getting older, moody older man, unsure about retirement, vague retirement plan

7 SNAKE: Scandalous older woman, resentment lasts a lifetime, lying older woman, jealous older woman, toxic elder, difficult senior lady, complicated retirement, enemies for life, cheating with an older woman

8 COFFIN: End of an era, slowing down with age, not private, dying elder, death of a father or grandfather, end of peace, silencing a senior, ill older man, expired, rest in peace, bad experience, dying of old age, no privacy

9 BOUQUET: Beautiful senior, handsome older man, art connoisseur, enjoying retirement, wonderful lifetime, surprise retirement party, delightful elder

10 SCYTHE: Dangerous older man, wounded veteran, surgery on an older person, suddenly getting old, disturbing the peace, breaking a senior's privacy

11 WHIP: Sexually experienced, arguing with an older man, sex with someone much older, critical of old people, sexual privacy, abusive father, sexually mature, active senior, lifelong abuse, sexual discretion

12 BIRDS: Older couple, talking for a while, discussing retirement, gossiping discreetly, talking privately, older sibling, gossip is getting old

13 CHILD: Grandchild, new experience, vulnerable elder, naive older man, short winter, beginning retirement, innocent senior

14 FOX: Cunning older person, sly old man, job privacy, retirement, scheming older man, manipulating older person, working at the same job until retirement, working with seniors, scamming a senior

15 BEAR: Grandmother, food connoisseur, resourceful elder, powerful older woman, boss is retiring, big discretion needed

16 STARS: Blessed lifetime, wishing to retire, online discretion needed, famous older man, inspiring elder, online privacy, eternal peace

17 STORK: Progressing calmly, change of seasons, changes last a lifetime, change brings about peace, nurturing father, gracefully aging, tall elder

18 DOG: Assisted living, reliable father, support for seniors, loyal older man, friendship lasts a lifetime, trail ran cold (investigation), protective elder

19 TOWER: Official retirement, lonely man, established senior, mandatory retirement, stubborn old man, withdrawn senior, arrogant old man

20 GARDEN: Meeting an older man, group of seniors, public retirement, world peace, public discretion, club for seniors, event for seniors, online group for seniors

21 MOUNTAIN: Barrier to retirement, delaying retirement, stone cold, obstacle to peace, harsh winter, obstacles throughout life, restriction

22 PATHS: Decision lasts a lifetime, indecisive elder, unfamiliar old person, road to peace, separated older couple, choices are lasting, planning retirement, different kind of retirement

23 MICE: Wearing down in old age, expiring soon, diminishing peace, dissolving privacy, past due, spoiling serenity, dirty old man

24 HEART: Relationship experience, loving older couple, loving winter, adoring father, doting grandfather, fulfilled lifetime, loving retirement, love lasts a lifetime, relationship privacy, loving an older man

25 RING: Commitment lasts a lifetime, married older man, vows last a lifetime, continual serenity, married later in life, dedicated older man, continued peace

26 BOOK: Great knowledge, secret kept a lifetime, extreme privacy, discretion, wise with age, a tome, extreme secrecy, expert, wisdom comes from life experience

27 LETTER: Message from an older man, communicating privately, archives, communication turns cold, letter from a senior, messages are old

28 MAN: Father, father figure, grandfather, older man, experienced man, wise man, "silver fox," private man, pensioner, calm man, mature man, retired man, cold man, discreet man

29 WOMAN: Older lady, experienced woman, wise woman, private woman, pensioner, peaceful lady, calm woman, mature woman, retired woman, cold woman, discreet lady, silver-haired lady

31 SUN: Success comes later in life, happy retirement, good age, melting snow, courageous senior, success lasts a lifetime, truthful older man, happy old age, a holiday north

32 MOON: Creative senior, emotional elder, feeling old, intuitive elder, meditation, feeling serene, shaman, crone, emotionally mature

33 KEY: Freedom with age, important older man, finding peace, unlocking wisdom, purposeful lifetime, destined old couple, influential older man, distinguished old man, of significant age

34 FISH: Inheritance, sugar daddy, financially experienced, budget, shopping for antiques, golden handshake, financial discretion required, business passed down generations, antiquing, business advice, business mentor

35 ANCHOR: Unchanged, long-lasting peace, settling down, calm, stability, secure and private, settling into retirement

36 CROSS: Burdened by age, painfully aging, difficult old person, dependent on others, hating the cold, obligated privacy, codependent senior, remorseful senior, obligation lasts a lifetime, disappointed by age

Time is jealous of you, and wars against your lilies and roses.
—Oscar Wilde

31 Sun

Bright burning flames, the heat of the fire
The truth will shine through, exposing the liar
Warmth on your face, of the Sun's golden rays
Renewal of joy, reminiscent of long summer days

KEYWORDS:

Energy, Truth, Vitality, Success, Renewal, Achievement, Positive outcome, Warm, Happiness, Confidence, Optimism, Summer, Light, Victory, Joy, Energy, Day, Win, Thrive, Consciousness, Golden, Renewal, South, Hot, Courage, Illumination, Radiance, Holiday/vacation, Good

MEANING:

The Sun is about the present, bringing rays of warmth and great joy. The Sun is a very positive card heralding only good things to come, and having a positive effect on all surrounding cards. The Sun can also denote a vacation somewhere warm, for some fun in the sun.

Lenormand Sun Combinations

1 RIDER: Other Man is good, declaring victory, arrival of summer, declaring the truth, speedy recovery, visit is optimistic, news is joyful, arrival of illumination, a youthful energy

2 CLOVER: Great fortune, fun in the sun, Lady Luck shines, St. Patrick's Day, fortunate outcome, pot of gold, happy days, brief, illumination, chance for success, happiness, cheerful, fun vacation, brief holiday, "it's your lucky day!"

3 SHIP: Trip somewhere warm, holiday, discovering the truth, traveling during the day, a journey south, exploring the truth, exploring consciousness, good-bye summer

4 HOUSE: Family success, housewarming, family victory, family day, domestic bliss, real estate success, home's electrical system, family truth, house energy, family vacation, staycation

5 TREE: Health renewed, spiritual light, healthy, healing rays of the sun, healing energy, recovery, growing warmer, tree lights, spiritual consciousness, spiritual energy, slow illumination, natural tan

6 CLOUDS: Clouding the truth, cloudy day, confusing outcome, rainy day, shade, depressed everyday, confusing energy, hiding the truth, unable to see good, stormy weather, obscuring the truth, fear of success

7 SNAKE: Problems in paradise, twisting the truth, lies illuminated, lying everyday, seductive energy, envious of success, cheating everyday, exotic holiday, needing a vacation

8 COFFIN: Eclipse, neutral, maybe, end of good times, empty win, negative energy, bad vacation, no joy, closed-off energy, the end of the day, negative outcome, no illumination (darkness), end of consciousness, blackout (loss of consciousness), burying the truth, canceled holiday

9 BOUQUET: Extreme happiness, beautiful day, renewal, joy, pleasant vibes, beautiful energy, perennials, enjoying success, wonderful summer, very positive outcome, luxury vacation, nice holiday, sweet success

10 SCYTHE: Cutting truth, dangerous energy, sudden success, cutting vacation short, dangerous truth, tie (dividing the win), dangerous outcome

11 WHIP: Back-to-back wins, questioning the truth, question of the day, aggressive energy, hedonistic vacation, flickering lights, bending the truth, questioning happiness, sexual vigor, arguing everyday

12 BIRDS: Speaking the truth, couple of passengers, nervous energy, couple's vacation, ungrounded energy, telling the truth, tourists, sibling energy, excited to fly somewhere warm

13 CHILD: Newfound confidence, small win, child energy, short summer, new consciousness, immature energy, short holiday, starting vacation

14 FOX: Cunning victory, workday, employment success, manipulating the truth, fake tan, sneaky energy, guilty conscious, working vacation, pretense of success, manipulating energy

15 BEAR: Immense joy, big win, powerful energy, powerful victory, powerful truth, big holiday, overly confident

16 STARS: Dreams come true, clear conscience, improving every day, twilight, dream vacation, highly successful, very positive, higher consciousness, electrical system, starlight, positive energy, exposing the truth, positive outcome, clear winner

17 STORK: Moving ahead, everyday, birthday, annual event, moving south, pregnancy success, moving day, change brings success, conceiving on vacation

18 DOG: Friendly win, friendship renewed, smell of success, dog days of summer, friendly energy, every dog has his day, reliable success, guiding light

19 TOWER: Official win, aloof energy, glory days, statutory holiday, recanting the truth, political win, proud of success, independently successful

20 GARDEN: Public holiday, team win, gathering during the day, public truth, group vacation, gathering energy, faith in society renewed, social-media success, collective consciousness

21 MOUNTAIN: Hard-won victory, impeded success, harsh truth, delayed success, obstacles to happiness, blocked energy, postponing your vacation

22 PATHS: Multiple victories, possibility of success, decision is good, free will, planning a holiday, road to success, path to happiness

23 MICE: Robbed blind, stolen victory, ruined day, steal my sunshine, draining energy, sunset (the setting sun), eating away at your confidence, worried every day, stress of success, stealing electricity, dirty truth, stressful holidays, ruined holiday

24 HEART: Heartwarming, romantic bliss, Valentine's Day, love's renewed, extreme happiness, heartfelt joy, loving life, loving energy, compassionate warmth, very fortunate, romantic vacation, confident lover

25 RING: Vow renewal, "ring of fire," continued success, contract awarded, promise of success, the Sun, committed to happiness, circle of trust, all-inclusive vacation, wedding day, honeymoon

26 BOOK: Secret of success, graduation, school holiday, educational success, Remembrance Day, educational achievement, researching vacations, memories come to light, searching for the truth

27 LETTER: Sending messages every day, results are optimistic, message of the day, sending light, message of relief, card of the day, message is true

28 MAN: Masculine, successful man, warm man, energetic man, optimistic man, courageous man, good man, confident man, truthful man, male energy

29 WOMAN: Successful woman, warm woman, energetic woman, optimistic lady, courageous woman, good woman, confident lady, truthful woman, female energy

30 LILY: Retirement bliss, snowbirds, old truth, lifetime achievement, father energy, lukewarm, winter holiday, snow day!

32 MOON: Enlightenment, solar eclipse, moon phase energy, illumination, emotional day, dusk, manifesting success, opposites, Monday, equinox, moonlight, illusion of truth

33 KEY: Open to joy, revealed in the light of day, answer of the day, karmic truth, answering truthfully, significant victory, unlocking the truth, important outcome, notable success, important win, definitely Yes!

34 FISH: Business success, financial win, shopping confidently, gold, deep joy, fishing vacation, flowing energy, fiscal year, expensive vacation, liquid courage, financially successful

35 ANCHOR: Long-term success, routine win, stuck energy, grounding energy, stable success, safe holiday, foundation to success, solid confidence, long-lasting happiness

36 CROSS: Disappointment, critical heat, obligated every day, painful day, worshiping the Sun, a sprit, testing your confidence, faith renewed, exhausted everyday, supernova, regretting the truth, difficult day

A smile is the same as sunshine; it banishes winter from the human countenance. —Victor Hugo

32 Moon

Mysteriously glowing silver orb, Full Moon in her prime
Rising in the inky darkness, a Triple Goddess so divine
Phases and aspects churning, tides and emotions felt so deep
Dreamy moonbeams surround you, casting shadows while you sleep

KEYWORDS:

Night, Manifestation, Emotions, Creativity, Intuition, Reflection, Feelings, Imagination, Subconscious, Magick, Appearance, Influence, Phases, Occult, Awareness, Talent, Divination, Fantasy, Skill

MEANING:

When the Moon card appears, she influences your emotions with her many faces. She will affect all the cards next and surrounding her. She brings a touch of mysticism and intuition, enveloping you in her magickal aura.

Lenormand Moon Combinations

1 RIDER: Speedy manifestation, receiving an intuitive message, teen witch, visitors show up, suitor is manifesting, youthful appearance, the maiden

2 CLOVER: Whimsy, the fey and elementals, lucky intuition, brief influence, lucky phase, joyful feeling, gambling skills, luck is manifesting, gambling phase, good-luck spell, flash of intuition, lucky feeling, a talisman

3 SHIP: Exploring intuition, travel spell, traveling at night, traveling phase, foreign influence, navigating feelings, exploring creativity, journey into your subconscious

4 HOUSE: Family influence, home protection spell, a hearth witch, cups, cottage magick, family coven, sacred space (indoor), brand awareness, real estate skills, comfortable feeling, homey feeling

5 TREE: Female reproductive system, hormones, wands, growing influence, health spell, medical intuitive, deeply rooted emotions, healthy imagination, waxing moon, blood moon, hereditary witch, palm reader, sanguine or blood magick, ancestral magick

6 CLOUDS: Mental health awareness, illusion, moodiness, magic (mundane kind), scary dream, sadness, delusion, confused feelings, storm moon, dark fantasy, hallucinations, telepathy, hidden feelings, temperamental, lunatic, meditation, turmoil

7 SNAKE: Jealousy, betrayed, lying about feelings, twisted emotions, attraction spell, Other Woman's influence, mesmerizing, alluring, complications with a spell, seductive skills, cheating phase, toxic emotions, complicated feelings, wicked spell

8 COFFIN: Grief, dead of night, dark moon, mediumship, mourning phase, necromancy, unconscious, no emotion, an apparition, unaware, mourning moon, a visitation, bad psychic, void of course moon, black magick, no imagination, negative spell (of ill intent), a ghost

9 BOUQUET: Gratitude, flower moon, sage, green witch, creative phase, glamour spell (beauty), melodramatic, herbal magick, Sabbat, smudging, gifted, artistic expression, constructing a spell, blossoming intuition, east quarter, herbs, beautiful crazy

10 SCYTHE: Hysterectomy, hurt feelings, dangerous spell, cut off emotionally, swords, harvest moon, athame, dangerous emotions, dangerous imagination, unexpected emotion, breaking (removing) a spell, gutted, west quarter

11 WHIP: Sexual fantasy, agitated feeling, sexual dream, sex magick, a pendulum, sexual phase, questionable influence, anger, violent feelings, active imagination, sex spell

12 BIRDS: Incantation, clairaudience, restless feeling, flighty, nervous, anxiety, neurotic, crow moon, music magick, calling the quarters, blue moon, musically inclined

13 CHILD: New moon, awkward feelings, immature phase, new talent, undeveloped skills, child's imagination, a poppet, micromoon

14 FOX: Job skills, manipulating emotions, cleaver, shrewd awareness, employment spell, working creatively, guilt, cleverness, instinctive feeling, fraudulent psychic, working a spell, guilty feeling, hocus-pocus

15 BEAR: Deep sleep, powerful feelings, power spell, clairgustance, overbearing emotions, kitchen witch, diet phase, the Mother, supermoon

16 STARS: "Make a wish!," intuitive, hopeful, pentacles, inspired, clairvoyance, astrology, uplifting emotions, tech witch, zodiac, lucid dreaming, manifestation, astrologer, positive influence, astral magick, astral plane (where you dream), north quarter, cosmic witch, fame

17 STORK: Fertility spell, telekinesis, baby moon, recurring dream, poltergeist, changing feelings, return-to-sender spell, birthing spell, evolving intuition, changeling

18 DOG: Trust your intuition, puppy phase, loyalty spell, clairalience, wolf moon, a familiar, a fletch, pet psychic, protection spell, trust your feelings!

19 TOWER: Watchtowers, legal spell, traditional witch, lonely feeling, solitary witch, self-aware, ridged appearance, controlling emotions, self-reflection

20 GARDEN: Meeting at night, coven, group influence, party all night, public awareness, group spell, hedgewytch, garden magick, sacred space (outdoor), pink moon, green thumb, psychic fair

21 MOUNTAIN: Blocked emotions, harsh appearance, stubborn feelings, blocked intuition, buck moon, permanent influence, runes, crystals, hard phase, rough skills

22 PATHS: Indecisive, decision was influenced, very unusual, falling apart (emotionally), unfamiliar spell, multiple spells, path to magick, planning phase, possibility of manifesting, eclectic witch, paranormal

23 MICE: Worried, destructive emotions, waning moon, diminished feelings, dirty appearance, obsessed, spoiled night, dwindling skills, less creativity

24 HEART: Loving feeling, passion, generous, cups, love magick, heartfelt emotions, dating phase, sensitive, tasseography (cup reading), empathic, love spell, clairsentience, romantic fantasy

25 RING: Full moon, commitment is manifesting, contract influence, intuitive connection, honeymoon, binding spell, circle casting, continual reflection

26 BOOK: Secret feelings, upgrading your skills, secret spell, Akashic records, studying the occult, studying witchcraft, researching spells, wisdom of the occult, Book of Shadows (BOS), grimoire

27 LETTER: Tarot, oracle, Lenormand, playing cards, cartomancy, written spell, automatic writing, sending a spell, message brings awareness, sigils

28 MAN: Creative man, emotional man, intuitive man, talented man, moon-faced man, compelling man, fantasy man, sensitive man, male witch, skillful man, man in the moon

29 WOMAN: Feminine, creative lady, emotional woman, intuitive woman, moon-faced woman, compelling woman, fantasy woman, sensitive woman, female witch, talented woman

30 LILY: Sentimental feeling, wise woman, an old spell, older appearance, the crone, mature feelings, cold moon, on a winter's night, calm, experienced

31 SUN: Daydreaming, good night, balanced, yin and yang, candle magick, optimistic feeling, warm feeling, brilliant creativity, truth spell, bright talent, good feeling, good phase, opposites attract, good dream, hot moon, summer nights, vibration, solstice, energy reader, energy magick, south quarter, confidence spell

33 KEY: Key phase, new way revealed, claircognizance, karmic influence, opening up emotionally, revealing a spell, unlocking the subconscious, important skill set, ceremonial magick, ritual

34 FISH: Business savvy, professional psychic, under the influence, sturgeon moon, deep reflection, flowing intuition, money spell, money is manifesting, business influence, business spell, deep feelings

35 ANCHOR: Stable influence, stuck emotions, serious feelings, persistent feelings, knot spell, drawing down the moon, grounding, sea witch

36 CROSS: Religious fanatic, unorthodox, religious phase, difficult emotions, painful reflection, religious dream, worshipping the moon, exorcist, Wicca, paganism, difficult spell, hex, omen, consecrating, curse, difficult night

Always remember we are under the same sky,
looking at the same moon. —Maxine Lee

33 Key

A destiny so noble, one Skeleton Key to open all
Karmic Fate interwoven, sewn into the fabric of your soul
A new opening is revealed, step into the great expanse
And become an active player, in this great Game of Chance

KEYWORDS:

Unlocking, Significant, Karmic, Important, Distinguished, Destiny, Fate, Noble, Solution, Ceremony, Access, Affirmative, Answers, Way out, Definite, Revealing, Open, Resolution, Freedom, Ritual, Honor, Respect, Yes

MEANING:

As one of the positive cards in the deck, when the Key appears it represents answers, with the possibility to unlock and open many opportunities both mundane and spiritual. If the Key could speak, it would give you a resounding "YES!"

Lenormand Key Combinations

1 RIDER: Newsworthy, getting answers, arrival of karma, quick fix, receiving access, suitor gives an answer, visit from fate, speedy access, caller of destiny

2 CLOVER: Small opportunity revealed, lucky destiny, kismet, happy synchronicities, easy access, gambling with fate, temporary freedom, informal ceremony, casual answer, serendipity

3 SHIP: Exploring freedom, discovering destiny, travel ritual, moving toward resolution, moving through, international access, navigating new ways

4 HOUSE: Property access, real estate answers, home page access, family celebration, family resolution, family access, family karma, family honor

5 TREE: Health answers, extended access, natural remedy, wellness is the focus, spiritually open, growth revealed, spiritual insight, ancestral karma, medical explanation, noble ancestors, natural opening, medical cure

6 CLOUDS: Needing clarification, confusing answers, hidden access, interference, hidden solution, fearing karma, troubling explanation, obscured destiny

7 SNAKE: Betrayal revealed, twist of fate, poser, problematic answer, lying about a solution, transformative answer, complicated solution, issues with access

8 COFFIN: Important ending, maybe, death rites, funeral, denied access, last rites, ill fated, significant end, final answer, bad karma, closed door, closing ceremonies, death is the only way out, no solution, the in-between (closed and open)

9 BOUQUET: Significant gift, beautiful ceremony, RSVP, beautiful destiny, embellished answers, appreciating freedom, occasion to celebrate, pleasant reply, wonderful solution, high-end fashion, acclaimed art, wonderful fate

10 SCYTHE: Instant karma, reap what you sow (karma), cutting off access, disrupting a ceremony, dangerous solution, unexpected explanation, turning point, dangerous access, autumn access

11 WHIP: Sexual freedom, hit with karma, questioning fate, abusive reply, repeated access, threat to freedom, questionable solution, rehearsed answer, habitual response, hurtful answer, angry response

12 BIRDS: Conversation is revealing, gossiping openly, talking freely, speaking openly, discussing a solution, verbal response, couple of solutions, hectic ceremony, couple is destined

13 CHILD: New revelation, small ceremony, new resolution, small significance, new access, immature answer, short explanation, simple solution, playing with fate

14 FOX: Wrong door, sneaking out, crafty solution, manipulating an answer, employment answer, work solution, finding a way out, suspicious answer, a witty response

15 BEAR: Powerful karma, big reveal, boss provides a solution, massive importance, huge celebration, powerful destiny, aggressive response, big honor

16 STARS: Wishing for resolution, it's fated, fame, highest honor, highly acclaimed, wishes granted, everything will be revealed, dreams will be attained, star-studded celebration, highly esteemed, highly important, positive response, destiny, electronic key

17 STORK: Moving toward resolution, change brings about a solution, recurring karma, spring access, move made is important, change is the answer

18 DOG: Friendship is destined, a friend has the answers, guided by destiny, friendly resolution, friend will reveal a new way, protecting freedom, trust the answer!

19 TOWER: Official answer, legal access, official response, respected organization, official ceremony, formal celebration, past-life karma, a formal reply

20 GARDEN: Meeting openly, public access, public ceremony, public response, gathering openly, teamwork is paramount, common response, public celebration, outdoor ceremony, all-access pass

21 MOUNTAIN: Obstacle to freedom, hard revelations, restricted access, harsh answers, limited access, blocking the way out, determined to challenge fate, remote access

22 PATHS: Decision is fated, multiple openings, many ways, path leads to the way out, road to freedom, choosing honor, road leads to destiny, unusual explanation, planning a celebration, choosing your destiny

23 MICE: Stolen access, fading importance, be vigilant and lock your doors, ruined reputation, taking away freedom, less and less access

24 HEART: Relationship answers, love revealed, love is the answer, significant relationship, lover revealed, love is fated, loving response, relationship is destined

25 RING: Marriage ceremony, what goes around comes around (karma), continued access, wedding celebration, offer is answered, proposal is answered, connection is key, connection is karmic, deal is destined

26 BOOK: Information is key, knowledge is freeing, secret reply, secret access, secret knowledge, secret rite, graduated with distinction/honors, convocation ceremony, graduation ceremony

27 LETTER: Written permission, communication opens up, noteworthy, writing your own destiny, result is positively Yes!

28 MAN: Free man, important man, soulmate, distinguished man, significant man, open man, virtuous man, influential man, key man, honorable man, available man, sophisticated man, nobleman, dignified man

29 WOMAN: Regal woman, free woman, important woman, soulmate, unforgettable woman, significant female, open woman, influential lady, key female, honorable woman, available woman, sophisticated woman, dignified lady, prestigious woman, noblewoman

30 LILY: Peace brings freedom, old resolution, private access, retirement celebration, private ceremony, winter access, retirement

31 SUN: Good karma, happy celebration, morning ritual, grand achievement, victory is assured, the "Yes!" card, truth is revealed, great solution, good answer, summer access

32 MOON: Emotionally open, feeling intuitively guided, nightly ritual, magickal ritual, prophecy, psychic access, precognitive dreams, the great rite

34 FISH: Financial access, business solutions, financial freedom, financial answers, abundance, flowing with destiny, wealthy

35 ANCHOR: Long-lasting solution, safe explanation, steady access, long karmic effects, routine response, safe way out, solid answer, securing your freedom

36 CROSS: Burdened by the revelation, disappointing truth, religious ceremony, prayers answered, painful destiny, sacrifice, experiencing the effects of karma, holy rite, difficult fate

Belief is the magic key that unlocks your dreams.
—Orrin Woodward

34 Fish

Deep in blue waters, abundance will flow
Budgeting and investing, making money grow
Business and commerce, an exchange of wealth
But drinking like a Fish is bad for your health

KEYWORDS:

Money, Flow, Commerce, Deepest, Business, Exchange, Alcohol, Shopping, Currency, Body of water, Prosperity, Wealth, Finance, Investments, Earnings, Abundance, Actual fish, Assets, Budget, Flow, Funds, Circulation, Transaction, Cost, Wages, Commissions, Resources

MEANING:

When the Fish comes swimming into you life, it denotes a feeling of going with the flow. Fish represent money; anything to do with finances, earnings, or transactions; and the movement of money in all its forms, including business and enterprise.

Lenormand Fish Combinations

1 RIDER: News exchanged, delivery of money, rushing water, declaring funds, arrival of cash, courier service business, quick cash, visiting a business

2 CLOVER: Lucky money, short-term investment, gambling on an investment, gambling money, gaming business, fortunate exchange, small sum of money, lucky investment, carefree spending, chance to earn, passive income

3 SHIP: Foreign investments, travel business, global business, journey over water, transferring money, trading account, international trade, trading stocks, foreign currency, traveling costs

4 HOUSE: Real estate investment, household budget, backyard swimming pool, real estate agency, real estate fund, real estate transaction, real estate resources, family money, real estate commissions, household purchase, home-based business, property value

5 TREE: Growing business, health-and-wellness business, robust finances, growing investment, wellspring (healing waters), growing funds, strong business, yoga flow, strong cash flow, health costs, life savings, interest (on money)

6 CLOUDS: Troubles in business, hidden account, rainy-day fund, hiding cash, alcoholism, hidden depths, sad finances, troubling finances, hidden costs, hiding purchases

7 SNAKE: River, problematic business, lying about finances, needing money, bribe, tempted by cash, lying about money, problems with plumbing, flexible income, seduced by money

8 COFFIN: Bankruptcy, funeral business, closing up shop, inheritance, depleted funds, no money, funeral costs, empty coffers, closed investment, buried treasure, lost wages, estate sale, death benefit

9 BOUQUET: Beauty or fashion business, enjoy spending money, spa business, surprise cash, seed money, the sweet smell of money, floral business, attracting abundance

10 SCYTHE: Dangerous investment, cut your losses, slashing prices, collections (money), severance pay, a budget (cutting costs), risky business, dicey investment, unexpected cash, cutting off the money, dividing assets

11 WHIP: Arguing about money, abusing finances, sexual exchange, hooker (sex for money), questioning finances, personal training or gym business, sex business, fighting over money

12 BIRDS: Discussing finances, gossiping about money, anxious about finances, discussing investments, partner's finances, talking shop, piano bar, music business

13 CHILD: New business, play money, kiddie pool, small investment, vulnerable business, small business, little cash, underage drinking, new money, start-up funds, irresponsible spending, new resources, small fee, small commission

14 FOX: Work wages, scammed out of money, manipulating finances, work wages, underhanded earnings, fraud, suspicious funds, scam business, counterfeit money, Ponzi scheme, used for money, fraudulent funds, fraudulent business

15 BEAR: Strong bottom line, powerful resources, bear market, substantial funds, profit, increased revenue, big money, large body of water, capital accumulation, strong portfolio, the boss, entrepreneur, big investment, grocery shopping

16 STARS: Wishing for abundance, online business, famous business, unlimited resources, potential earnings, online money, electrical current, e-transfer (electronic transfer), fame and fortune, positive cash flow, hopeful investment, online shopping

17 STORK: Seasonal business, exchange, moving money, nest egg, building a business, changing business, birth of a company, change in finances, exchanging money, relocating a business, returning a purchase, allocating resources, go with the flow!

18 DOG: Trust fund, reliable earnings, watch spending, support payments, insurance, protecting investments, dependable funds, pet business, protecting finances, watch investments, follow the money, audit

19 TOWER: Authorized funds, official allowance, legitimate funds, shopping center, government spending, corporate spending, legal business, past financial transactions, bank, financial institution, vault, authorized spending

20 GARDEN: Public funds, meeting at the pub, customers, public company, public pool, group funds, garden fountain, garden business, pooling funds

21 MOUNTAIN: Stagnant business, blocked cash flow, limited cash, budget, insurmountable debt, delayed funds, delayed payment, interrupted flow, restricted funds, holding back funds, blocked revenue, setback in business, limited resources

22 PATHS: Possibility to earn, choosing investments, multiple businesses, alternate funds, multiple sources of income, strange spending habits, many investments, multiple bank accounts, unusual transactions

23 MICE: Embezzlement, robbery, diminished earnings, losing a business, stealing money, worried financially, a corrupt business, dirty money, withdrawing money, depleted funds, costly (not necessarily money), vanishing resources, downsizing a business, losing money, ruining the business, corruption

24 HEART: Loving exchange, passionate about business, generous spending, philanthropy, loving deeply, charitable donations, for the love of money, love shopping, love spending

25 RING: Marital assets, ring shopping, IOU (promised money), ring exchange, wedding budget, marrying money, offer of money, contracting business

26 BOOK: Book exchange, book of business, secret funds, studying finance, secret cash, book commissions, smart investment, secret business, books of a business, under-the-table money, bookkeeper, information exchanged, secret ledgers, closet drinker, secret bank account

27 LETTER: Receipts, messages exchanged, checks, invoice, bills, chattel, letter of credit, cash (paper money), notice of assessment, certificate of holdings, sending money

28 MAN: Materialistic man, business man, entrepreneur, money man, wealthy man, independent man, man with deep pockets, alcoholic, investor, resourceful man

29 WOMAN: Material girl, business woman, entrepreneur, wealthy lady, independent woman, gold digger, woman with a big purse, alcoholic, investor, resourceful woman

30 LILY: Old money, established business, private funds, careful spending, established wealth, retirement fund, cold water, old investment, experienced business owner, cold fish, calm waters, pension, discreet finances, frozen assets

31 SUN: Successful business, confident spending, improving financial position, windfall (winning some money), relief fund, holiday money, vacation fund, good investment, holiday shopping, good fishing, hot water, good with money, successful investment

32 MOON: Emotional rush, emotional exchange, manifesting money, moonshine, creative business, emotional shopping, emotional investment, creative resources, psychic business, influenced by money

33 KEY: Open water, revealing finances, significant wealth, important investment, open investment, karmic debt, opening an account, free of debt, access to accounts

35 ANCHOR: Stable business, secure funds, steady wages, coastal waters, secure transaction, fixed investment, securing cash, deep pockets, stable finances, locked-in investment, fixed income, down by the water, steady flow, steady income, secured financing, secure investment, securities, long-term investment

36 CROSS: Overwhelming exchange, stress test, disappointing bank account, exhausting all finances, suffering financially, cosigner, obligated debt, burdened by business, painful exchange, debt, taxes

Bait the hook well. This fish will bite.
—William Shakespeare

35 Anchor

My little boat is adrift on life's vast ocean
Stopping for a little bit, suspending all motion
Lasting heaviness I feel and constantly endure
Dropping Anchor for a rest, now safe and secure

KEYWORDS:

Stability, Long lasting, Settling, Fixed, Safe, Coastal, Heavy, Bottom, Secure, Routine, Constant, Persistent, Unchanged, Enduring, Solid, Grounding, Steady, Hold, Mariner, Stuck, Down, Foundation, Dependable, Serious

MEANING:

When the Anchor drops into your life, it brings an energy of stability, something currently fixed in your life. There is a feeling of weightiness attached to the Anchor card, and it can denote that something is stuck in your life, but not for long, for you can always lift the Anchor.

Lenormand Anchor Combinations

1 RIDER: Announcement on hold, news anchor, visitors stay a while, activity is settling down, news is unchanged, delivery is held up, horse stable, young man is stable

2 CLOVER: Momentarily stuck, short-term stability, gambling routine, luck lasts for a while, win is secure, luck is reinforced, casual routine

3 SHIP: Harbor, marina, port, traveling constantly, navy, travel insurance, trip to the coast, car insurance, movement is settling down, ship's anchor, disembark, travel routine, run aground, boat in the harbor

4 HOUSE: Family stability, real estate on hold, family routine, house is solid, house is safe, refuge, very settled, home's foundation, family settling in, home insurance, family safety, building is secure, domestic security, home page security, basement

5 TREE: Extremely stable, medical procedure on hold, health is stable, earthing, roots, healthful routine, life insurance, health insurance, putting your life on hold, enduring, spiritually grounded

6 CLOUDS: Unstable, addiction lingers, fear settles in, uncertainty, storm persists, feeling down, confusion persists, depression is heavy, doubt settling in, unstable foundation, mentally stuck, disturbance lasts, tempest in the harbor

7 SNAKE: Problems linger, lying constantly, cheating persists, desire endures, wires down, betrayal is long lasting, enemy's hold, Other Woman is persistent

8 COFFIN: End of stability, burial, dead serious, letting go, illness persists, silence lingers, releasing the anchor, 6 feet under, negativity persists, grief persists, coma

9 BOUQUET: Event on hold, beauty lasts, alleviating heaviness, beauty routine, partying constantly, East Coast, beauty procedure on hold

10 SCYTHE: Surgery on hold, danger lingers, crack in the foundation, severing ties, breaking the monotony, suddenly on hold, dangerous routine, West Coast, cutting anchor, reckless, autumn lingers

11 WHIP: Exercise routine, arguments persist, abuse is constant, abuse is lingers, assault is serious, conflict lasts, violence is ongoing

12 BIRDS: Partnership endures, gossip lingers, anxiety persists, hectic routine, planes are grounded, conversation on hold, call on hold, bird sanctuary, nerves settle down, gossiping persists, negotiations are stuck, music is grounding

13 CHILD: Immaturity lasts, child safety, child settles, simple routine, weak foundation, new routine, weak hold, venerability remains

14 FOX: Career on hold, manipulation lasts, workplace routine, workplace insurance, job security, work is dependable, workplace safety, employment insurance, guilt persists

15 BEAR: Strong foundation, diet on hold, diet plateau, boss is dependable, powerful hold, manager is reliable, great stability, big and heavy

16 STARS: Goals secured, the north shore, online security, goal is solid, blessings last, positively safe, fame is long lasting, positive routine, eternally enduring, forever, immortal

17 STORK: Changing routine, move on hold, seasonal routine, movement, springtime lingers, progress, shifting the anchor, transition is stable, the move is safe

18 DOG: Steadfast, familiar routine, very dependable, friendship lasts, pet insurance, friendship endures, investigation put on hold, safe

19 TOWER: Loneliness lasts, strict routine, formally on hold, building is secure, the past lingers, laying down the foundation

20 GARDEN: Socializing constantly, social routine, public safety, social gatherings on hold, team is secured, group safety, crowd lingers, hangout

21 MOUNTAIN: Rock bottom, very stuck, permanent, not much movement, obstacles persist, delays last, challenge remains, fixed, challenging routine, not going anywhere

22 PATHS: Decision on hold, hesitation persists, choices weigh you down, no decision made, choices coming up, unusual routine

23 MICE: Lessening grip, worrying constantly, deteriorating, theft insurance, losing your footing, declining stability, unsafe, undependable, fading, hollow

24 HEART: Love lasts, relationship on hold, love endures, relationship is solid, passion remains, lover holds on, romance lingers

25 RING: Agreement stands, commitment lasts, settling down, contract is secure, binding, wedding on hold, handcuffs, ball and chain

26 BOOK: Secret routine, education on hold, information remains the same, knowledge is sound, secret is safe

27 LETTER: Paperweight, schedule on hold, messages persist, communication lingers, results have a lasting effect

28 MAN: Stable man, settled man, serious man, persistent man, safe man, secure man, grounded man, solid man, stuck man

29 WOMAN: Stable woman, settled female, serious woman, persistent woman, safe woman, secure lady, grounded woman, solid woman, stuck woman

30 LILY: Retirement on hold, established routine, winter lingers on, old-age security, the north shore, experiencing stability, peaceful pause

31 SUN: Daily routine, sundown, the south shore, good foundation, success lasts, holiday on hold, optimism endures, summer lingers on, energy is grounding

32 MOON: Nightly routine, emotionally stuck, emotionally secure, spell is long lasting, intuitively stuck, feeling stuck

33 KEY: Important routine, fate, karmic effects are long lasting, things open up, fate remains unchanged, destiny secured, key chain, access on hold

34 FISH: Money lasts, financially stable, deposit insurance, funds secured, business stability, business routine, funds on hold, business insurance, financial security

36 CROSS: Burdens weigh you down, a spirit lingers, pain is constant, warding off evil, burdens last, suffering constantly, obligation weighs you down, difficulties last

You're stronger than us. Once you find your anchor never let go of it. No matter what. —John Marrs

36 Cross

This burden I feel, so heavy in my heart
The bitter sorrow and pain just tears me apart
The hardship of life causes misery and despair
Trials and tribulations of the Cross that I bear

KEYWORDS:

Sacred, Burdens, Despair, Sorrows, Beliefs, Duty, Religion, a Spirit, Suffering, Hardships, an Alter, Pain, Intolerance, Obligation, Regret, Ideology, Tests, Crisis, Disappointment, Responsibility, Shame, Tax, Anguish, Faith, Exhausting, Burnout, Dogma, Misery, Worship, Difficulty, Victim, Fatigue

MEANING:

The Cross, being a negative card, comes into the reading bearing great hardships, burdens, and obligations. It is something that you will have to go through and endure.

Lenormand Cross Combinations

1 RIDER: Peddler of religion, visit is necessary, coming difficulties, news is disappointing, announcement brings obligations, a young spirit, visit is painful, disappointment looms in the horizon, delivering painful news

2 CLOVER: Brief suffering, relief from sorrow, easy test, easing obligation, alleviating pain, gaming tax, gambling shame, chance of burnout, temporary responsibility, a happy spirit

3 SHIP: Pilgrimage, missionary, exploring religion, trip is disappointing, journey of the soul, duty tax, drive test, transitioning through pain, travel exhaustion, foreign tax

4 HOUSE: House of pain, family crisis, property tax, a house spirit, home altar, family shame, real estate tax, family obligations, place of worship, family responsibility, family in pain

5 TREE: Aches and pains, exhaustion, earth-based religion, health crisis, body shame, health is suffering, health test, extended obligation, health tax, medical test

6 CLOUDS: Guilt, torment, mental anguish, mental strain, great despair, confused about religion, mental health crisis, mental health testing, mentally exhausted, hell, gloom and doom, unclear obligation, drug test, uncertain pain

7 SNAKE: Spiraling out of control, lying about suffering, troubling test, sacred, toxic shame, cheating on a test, Pentecostal religion (snake worship), Other Woman in crisis, complex beliefs, an alluring spirit, transformation is painful

8 COFFIN: Ending exhaustion, grief is burdensome, final rites, loss causes suffering, immense grief, loss of faith, death and taxes, ending hardships, buried grief, final test, death tax, a malevolent spirit

9 BOUQUET: Improvement, recovery, surprise test, gratitude, invitation to a place of worship, a beautiful spirit, blossoming faith, devotional, pleasant duty

10 SCYTHE: Suicidal, cutting taxes, sudden sorrow, surgical pain, a cult, collecting taxes, sudden pain, warning, stabbing pain, sudden exhaustion, a dangerous spirit

11 WHIP: Torture, physical abuse, sexual shame, rape, sexual duty, sexual crisis, sexual worship, physical exhaustion, repetitive suffering, an active spirit, arguing about religion, incubus or succubus, criticism, practice test, debating religion

12 BIRDS: Confessions, talk of sorrow, couple in crisis, like a prayer, gossip causes ruin, voice stain, discussing duties and responsibilities, conversation about taxes, oral test, distress, singing hymns, a chatty spirit, discussing religion

13 CHILD: Baptism/naming, child tax, growing pains, child in crisis, childhood shame, playing the victim, little suffering, child is exhausting, a child spirit, small test, tiny obligation, a little bit painful

14 FOX: Overworked, job causes suffering, work ethic, extreme workload, manipulating taxes, coworker in crisis, work duties, a manipulative spirit, employment difficulties, work fatigue

15 BEAR: Unbearable pain, boss in crisis, diet fatigue, big disappointment, food allergy test, big responsibility, huge obligation, fat shaming, great suffering, bearing down, big regret, a powerful spirit

16 STARS: Faith, high priest, high priestess, hope shines through, star worship, hopeful, epiphany, heaven, positive test, fame is exhausting, online test

17 STORK: Change causes pain, pregnancy test, leg pain, labor pains, changing your religion, seasonal suffering, rearranging duties, long test, shifting responsibilities, progressive pain

18 DOG: Priest, friendship is tested, dogma, Doberman pinscher, obligation, a friendly ghost, friend in crisis, friendship is exhausting, a helpful spirit, protection, helping a spirit cross over (rescue work)

19 TOWER: Towering crisis, corporate tax, cathedral, legal obligation, trial, back pain, government in crisis, formal obligation, official duty, government tax, an ancient spirit

20 GARDEN: Public crisis, garden temple, public suffering, public duties, taxes (public burden), public worship, public shaming

21 MOUNTAIN: Isolated pain, delayed suffering, postponing a test, insurmountable despair, impassive hardship, a stubborn spirit, hard obligation, harsh treatment, remote testing

22 PATHS: Multiple responsibilities, choice of duties, much suffering, decisions are exhausting, many regrets, multiple-choice test, polytheism, choice is painful, multiple spirits, many disappointments

23 MICE: Breakdown, cult, less responsibility, dwindling faith, costly sacrifice, drained, lessening the load, utter ruin, alleviating sorrows, dirty shame, obsessed with religion

24 HEART: Heartache, love is tested, heart wrenching, partner in crisis, relationship is suffering, affection is strained, dating is exhausting, loving worship, a loving spirit, relationship responsibility, relationship fatigue

25 RING: Marital duties, bound by suffering, ring of office, marriage is strained, commitment is exhausting, marriage regret, contract responsibilities, marriage in crisis, connecting with spirit, contractual obligation

26 BOOK: Book of worship, secret duties, educational load, unknown source of pain, secret worship, studying fatigue, secret shame, concealed pain, secret obligation, educational test, studying theology

27 LETTER: Written test, messages are painful, results are disappointing, messages from spirit, text is disappointing, schedule is grueling

28 MAN: Religious man, miserable man, tormented man, defeated man, afflicted man, needy man, pained man, obligated man, suffering man, burdensome man, remorseful man, difficult man, disappointing man, man in crisis, exhausted man, male spirit

29 WOMAN: Pious woman, miserable woman, tormented lady, defeated woman, remorseful woman, afflicted female, needy woman, pained woman, obligated woman, suffering female, burdensome woman, difficult woman, disappointing woman, woman in crisis, worn-out woman, a female spirit

30 LILY: Peace is disrupted, old obligation, winter blues, retirement hardship, old person in crisis, old pain, caregiver burnout, an old spirit

31 SUN: Recovery, relief, sunburn, good test, Sunday, improvement, sun god, day of worship, passing a test, sun worship, a benevolent spirit, heat exhaustion

32 MOON: Emotional pain, moon worship, feeling like a victim, influenced by religion, emotionally taxed, moon goddess, psychic pain, feeling obligated, psychic burnout

33 KEY: Solution is painful, significant responsibility, important duties, opening the door to spirit, important test, a free spirit, fate, karma is a bitch, free from obligation

34 FISH: Deep suffering, money woes, deep shame, financial crisis, business tax, income tax, financial test (stress test), business ethics, deep pain, buyer's remorse, financial struggle, financial obligation, financial strain, breathalyzer test, paying taxes

35 ANCHOR: Lasting pain, heavy burden, heavily taxing, weighed down, long-term suffering, serious regret, heavy shame, routine exhaustion

Life's not about how hard of a hit you can give . . .
it's about how many you can take and still keep moving forward.
—Sylvester Stallone, Rocky Balboa

The time has finally come to end this fantastical tale,
Weaved throughout the cards, of the mystery unveil.
36 unforgettable characters you've met along the way,
Whispering ancient wisdoms and cultivating word play.
Well-wishes as you go on and explore just a little more,
Lost in the Enchantment of Lenormand, the book of lore.

Love, Kalliope
The Muse of Epic Poetry

About the Authors

Named after the Muse of Epic Poetry, Kalliope was taught from a very young age to read cards from her grandmothers. This began her love of cartomancy and led her to reading cards professionally for more than 30 years. In her former life, she held careers in both hospitality and financial management until 2015, when she answered Spirits' call to share her innate intuitive gifts with the world. Kalliope is currently touring North America and is featured as an international psychic medium and cartomancer. When not on the road, living the gypsy life, you can find her at home in her pyjamas curled up on the couch with a pen in hand and writing. She lives with her Mr. and two teen boys in their lakeside home in Ontario, Canada.

Yasmeen Westwood is a self-taught photomanipulation artist living in Perthshire, Scotland, in the United Kingdom. She had always wished to be an artist but could not paint or draw. Then she came across Photoshop. Her passion for playing with images led to the creation of her first deck, The Tarot of Enchanted Dreams. She is a professional photographer who sees magic both in the people and landscapes she photographs. She loves taking images and manipulating them to create magical, fantasy worlds, and it is this magic that she has tried to depict in this Lenormand deck.